HOW TO BE AN OLD GUY

DISPATCHES FROM THE RETIREE FRONT

Large Print

How to be an
Old Guy

Bill Kilpatrick

Hatala Geroproducts • Greentop, Missouri

Published in the United States of America
by Hatala Geroproducts, Greentop, MO 63546

                                    (pop 427)

09 08 07 06 05 1 2 3 4 5

How to Be an Old Guy: Dispatches From the Retiree
Front
by Bill Kilpatrick

ISBN-13: 978-1-933167-34-3

LCCN: 2009923698

Cover Design: Charles Dunbar
Composition: Age Positive Editorial Services

"You know you're getting old when instead of a martini you'd rather have a dish of ice cream."
— Phyllis Kilpatrick

CONTENTS

FOREWORD

It has been said so often we tend not to pay attention to its very real truth; that getting old isn't for the timid or the faint of heart. To the contrary, as this most timely and admirable book points out, it's a battle (especially for men, in that women tend to carry on pretty much as they always have), an everyday struggle to stay as healthy as possible, to adjust to new routines, to maintain dignity, to have and hold onto a sense of self-worth, to lead a fulfilling and rewarding life.

One of the first things men have to recognize and accept as we approach old age is that things wear out and break down; we're not twenty-two anymore. The truly amazing mechanism that is our body starts to bang, and there's nothing we can do about it other than try to keep it in running order as long as possible. That's probably why, while we may forget how to get downtown, blindfolded we know how to get to the doctor's office. Like Jan Murray used to say, "If it weren't for doctor appointments I'd have no social life at all."

Another word combination we hear so often we tend to tune it out is "diet and exercise," yet both are important if we're to maintain some semblance of what we used to be.

As old men we have to get off the couch, both

mentally and physically. We have to take a walk, do a few mild exercises — whatever it takes to keep everything moving. Even in bed we can stretch our arms and legs, rotate our ankles, point our toes, wiggle our fingers. And we have to stay tuned to what's going on in the world, if only for the sake of intelligent conversation.

We have to watch what we eat, the idea being to not allow ourselves to become fat. We have to cut down on salt, pass up sodas, stick to lean cuts of meat, eat chicken and fish, green vegetables, fresh fruit. Personally, I eat a lot of tomato sauce, not on pasta, but as a sauce on just about everything short of ice cream. I find it's good for me, and although I'm 85, I'm happy to say I still enjoy my food; I get pleasure from sitting down to a meal, even if it's no more than a snack. Mainly, I like to think that when it comes to what I eat I use common sense.

There's no "cure" for finding yourself an old guy; nothing you can take to make it go away, but you can live with it, and live well at that. A big part of doing so is what goes on in your head; you're in charge of what you think, of your attitude, of how you react to people and events. As the author makes clear, the key is to not punish yourself, to enjoy what you have, to laugh a lot, avoid depression, and pay attention to yourself and to your relationships with others.

All this and a lot more of what should be of concern to old guys is covered in this handbook of plain, straight, and sincere old-guy-to-old-guy talk, written with a healthy dose of no baloney common sense and humor. Stressed by the author, for example, is the need to keep busy, to have something to do each day. As for me, for my sake and for that of my family I've got a full-time job, and that's taking care of myself. It pays pretty good, too.

Sid Caesar
Beverly Hills, California
February 2009

INTRODUCTION

Russian revolutionary Leon Trotsky was only sixty-one when in 1940 an assassin wielding an ice axe did him in, so he never got to experience first-hand the sagacity of a 1935 entry he made in his diary:

"Old age," noted Trotsky, "is the most unexpected of all things that happen to a man."

Were the old Bolshevik still among those present I could assure him that, indeed, any man who meets the definition of an old guy finds it hard to believe what has befallen him. Men, especially those who to one extent or another have been for most of their lives movers and shakers, and who may still have their noses to some form of grindstone, manage to place on hold the inevitability of time.

The shock of being an old guy can be and often is devastating, even for men who retain some degree of power over enterprises, people and events. It isn't a matter of facing the truth reflected in the mirror, or of needing dentures, or of experiencing lower back pains. It's not even the infuriating business of being patronized by those who are markedly younger. What really drives home the bitter truth of being an old guy is the realization of one's essential irrelevance.

There are exceptions, of course, men who in their

eighties and even beyond retain their celebrity, relevance, and sense of self-worth (television's Mike Wallace comes to mind). But what we have in mind here is the graying army of the obscure and the unknown, men who at one age or another retire and fade away to anonymity and insignificance, their past yesterday's bananas, their future a blank stretching for however long to their death.

Other than politicians soliciting their votes, or people trying to sell them something, no one much cares what old guys think, or how they feel. Even devoted wives fail to appreciate the absolutely crushing effect irrelevance has on a man. Old guys barking in indignation at television inanities, for example, are pigeon-holed as cranky curmudgeons, their families failing to recognize the barks as cries to be heard, to be of some significance in the headlong rush of time and events.

Often repeated is the truism that old age isn't for sissies. It isn't. Rather, it's a battle, a fight to verify one's being. What follows, then, is an attempt to prepare and arm old guys and pending old guys for the battle that lies ahead. The intent isn't to cover all contingencies; it is not nor is it intended to be an old age manual. But with any luck, those who already are old guys and those about to become old guys will find herein insights and encouragement intended to help them fight the good fight.

You'll note throughout minimal references to doctors, psychologists, sociologists, psychiatrists, social workers, clergymen, and the like, few of whom, at least in their professional capacities, have much of anything to pass along in the way of either solutions or advice. They get old, too, and wrestle with the same problems as does every other old guy. On the other hand there will be occasional references to things said or written by poets, lyricists, writers, philosophers, and just plain wise old men. Other inputs are my own and based on experience as well as a lot of conversation and a lot of hanging around with men of post-retirement age. Even bolstered by the thoughts and insights of such sources, however, the hard fact is this: The only one who can make being an old guy a worthwhile and rewarding, even pleasant experience is the old guy you see in your shaving mirror.

1

MAKING TIME YOUR ALLY

One of the really scary aspects of becoming an old guy is the sudden awareness there are hours in a day that somehow have to be filled. Once the morning coffee has been savored, the day stretches ahead, challenging us to make worthwhile use of it. If, even though an old guy, there's a business to attend to, an office to go to, a familiar routine to be followed, all well and good. But most old guys are retirees and have been cut adrift and, while they may not realize it when first new at that station in their lives, face an abyss. Time becomes a dragon that must be slain.

I live, work and play in Florida, where I'm surrounded by thousands and thousands of old guys, some of whom seem to be handling well the transition from job-filled days to optional leisure, others of whom are, figuratively, lost at sea. All of them presumably once had a retirement dream, but only a few have realized it. The others have been forced either to revise their original conceptions, or have dropped out to await, sourly more often than not, the Hooded Skeleton with the Scythe.

When I first moved to Florida from the suburbs of New York City I met and played golf with a doctor named Jack O'Brien. He's no longer among those present, but something he once told me has remained stuck in my mind. He said I'd be surprised at the high incidence of alcoholism among the community's retirees, men and the occasional woman who, unless they have something specific to do, by 11 o'clock most mornings are at least half-loaded. The typical pattern as he described it was that they then would stumble through lunch, throw themselves down and sleep it off, awake again late in the afternoon, whereupon they'd mix and stir a pitcher of martinis and re-load. At the time I found the specter of that terribly depressing, and I still do.

Even if old guys avoid the booze trap, they tend to fall victim to delusion, or, perhaps more properly, to myth. A few years before retirement they start making plans and counting the days. On the horizon they envision endless hours during which they plan to fish, play golf or tennis, swim, garden, mess around with a boat, go hunting, carve decoy ducks, entertain family and friends, play with their grandchildren . . . whatever. When at last they're cut loose they sell the house, pack up their stuff and relocate to Florida, Arizona, Southern California, an island in the Caribbean, a restored farm house in the Tuscan hills, a cottage in the countryside . . . wherever.

And then, before long, the rot starts to set in. They begin to appreciate the cruel juxtaposition of retirement and its promised leisure with advancing age. The thirty-five-year-old golf nut who dreams of one day having the leisure to play every day of his life finds out at age sixty-five that three or four consecutive eighteen-hole days not only is tiring but can become boring as well. The gardening buff works like a cotton picker getting everything dug up and planted, but once his various projects are completed — a process that because he has nothing else to do usually consumes considerably less time than anticipated — he wonders what next.

What's afoot here is that the pre-retirement man — actively employed, with a job to go to, a business to attend to, daily family life to be led — subconsciously looks upon his golf, his fishing, tennis, gardening or what-have-you as *recreation*, as time "stolen" from his purpose in life, which is to procreate and provide for and protect the family he has created. Such time is, then, mildly forbidden fruit and thus gratifying. Undoubtedly the caveman who paused from the hunt to rest under a tree while gnawing on an apple experienced like gratification.

But when what we think of as recreation becomes a time-filler rather than time "stolen" from life's purpose, the zing tends to fade, the deliciousness of the activity to go flat. Satiation rears its disquieting head, and the realization dawns that all such recreational activities can too easily exhaust their once promising attraction.

The reality of such a realization is expressed in a cartoon depicting an older couple at the breakfast table, its caption reading:

SHE: What are you going to do today, dear?
HE: Oh, I suppose play golf, dammit.

The fact is that to feel ourselves still active, still in the game, we need something going "against the grain." Day-to-day life as an endless idyll is life unbearable. The man who claims, then, to be carefree and not have a worry in the world is a mindless boob, and the man who can browse through a reasonably decent daily newspaper and not get from it something to make him smile, make him wonder, or trigger his indignation, simply isn't plugged-in. The beat of daily living doesn't cease because one becomes an old guy.

At one point in an admittedly checkered career I was a columnist for a daily newspaper in Florida. In that my presumed readers included many retirees, I made it a practice to stop by at least once a week at a local so-called senior center. My initial eager anticipation of such visits soon turned to dread, for seldom have I found myself in more depressing surroundings. Quite apart from the vague yet overriding smell of urine, the desperateness on the one hand and the lassitude on the other with which the center's regulars went about their activities would suggest the prudence of perhaps seeking out a revolver and a soundproof room.

I usually walked away from such visits with at least

something or someone to write about, but rarely with a bounce in my step. I kept thinking there has to be better things for these people to be doing than playing games, watching daytime television, learning and practicing essentially useless crafts, listening to guest speakers, being entertained by minor league (strictly so) folk singers, or taking part in seminars devoted to subjects about which they had to be only marginally interested. Society's rationale for such endeavors is, I suppose, it keeps the old folks off the streets and gives them a place to go where they can rub elbows with their age peers. That it's also a tragic waste of a valuable resource seemingly isn't considered.

It was my experience that the old gals encountered in the center did a better and personally more rewarding job of killing time than did the old guys. The women can always talk about a niece who lives in Des Moines, or about the grandchildren. Old guys, on the other hand, usually aren't all that gregarious, and after a few perfunctory exchanges with those around them tend to wind up sitting in silence.

I remember one guy sitting alone at a table in the center's cafeteria, an ashtray full of squashed butts in front of him, an opened pack of cigarettes off to one side. I stopped to chat with him, and it was like pulling teeth to get him to respond. But eventually he did, and what came out was pure bile — how he hated living in Florida, that he had nothing to do, that he had nothing in common with those around him, and on and on, all of it in a similar vein. In short, a most unhappy fellow.

Turned out he was from Brooklyn, where he had been born, grew up, and had spent his entire working life. He hadn't wanted to retire to Florida, but that's what his wife had in mind, so they packed up and ventured forth, pretty much their entire life's savings invested in a new and typical Florida two-bedroom, two-bathroom condominium. He wasn't a golfer, didn't care for fishing, had no hobbies, in truth hadn't anything to keep him from brooding about the hand life had dealt him. According to his account the couple bickered constantly, him regretting their move, her telling him to get used to it. But then she became ill and died, and not having anyone with whom to bicker, and were he to sell the condominium not having any place to go, not even back to Brooklyn, he was truly adrift, smoking himself to death and stewing in his own bitter juices. I remember coming home that night, putting my arms around my wife as she was preparing dinner and telling her how much I loved her.

When we first moved to Florida, and before we built our modest little house, my wife and I lived for a year or two in an apartment complex. A fellow resident of the complex was a guy named Lou who lived with a woman who may have been his wife. I've forgotten his last name, but he, too, was a New Yorker, a native Manhattanite who before moving to Florida lived in the East Side house in which he was born. He was a retired bailiff of the New York City court system and also the co-owner of a small cigar and newspaper stand on the Manhattan side of the Queensboro Bridge.

If ever a fish was out of water it was Lou in Florida. To him everything was "Amateur Night in Dixie." Nobody moved fast enough. His whole life had been the house in the East 60s, his job at 100 Centre Street (the New York City courthouse), the cigar and newspaper stand, a few neighborhood restaurants, and an occasional day at a New York area horse racing track or ballpark. He didn't last long, and within a year fled back to New York, perhaps leaving behind the woman with whom he had arrived. To this day I can hear him saying, repeatedly and indignantly, "What the hell's the matter with these people down here?"

I grant you neither of these men had much imagination, otherwise they'd have adapted, but my encounters with them drive home a point: Be certain to pick the right location in which to be an old guy.

Both would have been more successful as old guys had they remained among familiar surroundings. Arthur "Bugs" Baer, an old Hearstling, once wrote, "New York is New York, and every place else is Bridgeport." That's a New York frame of mind, and all the palm trees in the world aren't going to change it. The guys I've told you about, if they wanted a warm climate, should have been in Miami Beach, where a number of the inhabitants speak

New Yorkese and where you can get an authentic pastrami sandwich and a bottle of celery tonic.

What so many old guys fail to appreciate is that retirement is a whole new deal calling for often radical changes in lifestyle as well as considerable revisions in outlook. The retiree who strives to cling to what once was is doomed to fail, often miserably so. The trick, in effect, is to re-invent yourself, become the new and different person circumstances encourage you to become. If he's a plugged-in old guy, the avuncular school crossing guard who once owned and ran, say, a booming electrical supply company doesn't brood about his seeming reduction in status in the eyes of his community. Rather, he measures his value as a human being by doing a terrific job of being a school crossing guard.

The point is that old guys have to change if they are to find worthwhile the process of getting from one day to the next. It's a new you, and while your know-how and life experience may enable you to do a good job of whatever you decide to do to fill your days, what you once were you no longer are. Not in a religious sense, of course, but you are, in effect, re-born, and within recognized limitations (the state of your health and overall physical condition being paramount) the world is your oyster. You can do any damn thing you want to do and are capable of doing. Old guys who have done so successfully are among the most contented and most admired men I'm privileged to know. They include tutors, teacher assistants, hospital volunteers, clinical assistants, counselors of one stripe or another, school bus drivers, playground supervisors, landscaper helpers, patrollers of beaches . . . all men who in one way or another not only have a reason to get out of bed each morning, but who know in their bones they're still in the game, not in the major leagues, perhaps, but making worthwhile contributions to society.

One friend, a former book publishing executive who gave considerable thought to what he might like to do after reaching mandatory retirement age, found and bought himself an antique hand press as well as the old type faces that went with it, and had the lot of it lugged into the basement of his house. There, after spending a number of library hours doing the necessary research to learn how, and trying this and that, he restored the old press to working condition and cleaned up its type faces. Since, setting the type by hand as it has been done since the earliest days of mechanical printing, he has built up a small yet rewarding business doing odd jobs — bulletins, fliers, letterheads, envelopes, wedding announcements, invitations, and so on — for local community organizations and individuals who get a kick out of having their stuff printed in 19th century type faces. He doesn't advertise, doesn't need to, doesn't charge much; word-of-mouth has brought customers to him. He works when he feels like it, and when he does work, rarely more than few hours a day.

He spends the rest of his time (as he puts it) "puttering."

I'd be hard-pressed to define the word "happiness," but I suspect my friend at least has a handle on it. His days are full, he's doing something he likes doing, he works at his own pace, and he brings in the few extra dollars that enable him and his wife to spread their wings a little. He's no longer a pressured executive; rather, he's a printer, a craftsman who works with both his mind and his hands. What could be more rewarding than that?

2

Appearance and
Self-Respect

As the son of a golf course superintendent I knew as a small child what the word "seed" meant; it was sort of powdery stuff that came in cloth bags stacked in a corner of a barn at Sunningdale Country Club in Scarsdale, N.Y. I knew that every now and then some of the bags would be emptied into a spreader, which in turn would be pulled by a horse or a tractor over portions of the golf course. Either that or a bag or two would be broken into and the contents thereof scattered by hand and then hand-raked into a patch of raw ground. I understood that given water and appropriate nourishment the seed thus deployed would turn into grass, a process not terribly difficult for a five-year-old mind to grasp.

What threw me for a loop, however, was one day overhearing my mother, after returning from grocery shopping, telling my father that she had run into Mr. So-and-So, and that the poor old guy was looking rather seedy. I struggled with that one, mental pictures including an old man with grass growing out of his forehead and out of the backs of his hands. It was years before I understood what the term meant, that "looking seedy," or "has gone to seed" went hand-in-hand with "down-at-the-heel and out-at-the-elbow." Still years later the definition was extended to include shabby or soiled clothing, an unshaven face, a ratty-looking hat, perhaps even a face that could use a wash. And still more years later I came to appreciate that "looking seedy" was a trap into which old guys could easily fall, especially old guys who find themselves on their own.

"I mean, what the hell? Nobody's going to see me, right? So why should I shave? And this shirt is okay; I only wore it yesterday. I suppose these pants really should be dry-cleaned; maybe I'll take 'em in next week. Hey, wait, this hat's my favorite. So it's a little greasy and sweat-stained. So what? I don't go out of the house without it. Bought it ten years ago and have worn it ever since. These shoes? Yeah, I suppose they look kinda worn-out, but they're comfortable. Besides, I don't have to bend over to put 'em on."

Sound familiar? I hope not, for one of the sorriest and saddest of sights is a formerly neat fellow who as an old guy has allowed himself to "go to seed." Such a happening signifies not only complete withdrawal from the game, but also the surrender of self-esteem; the guy in the shaving mirror, then, even if glimpsed only occasionally, becomes a stranger, an unknown not only to the man he used to be but also to those who knew him before the seediness took root.

Even if you awake each morning alone and without a clue as to what you're going to do with the rest of the day, make it your very real business to attend to your ablutions — a shower (a daily habit, please, whether morning or at night), or at least washed face and hands, teeth brushed, hair combed, shaved, or if you have a moustache or beard making certain it's clean, combed or brushed, trimmed and neat. By such a simple routine will you set yourself for the day ahead, even should the day prove a dud. Keep in mind that it's important to be prepared at all times to meet head-on whatever comes along.

Not an exception at all is the old guy with a two-day growth of beard and dirty fingernails who throws on some indifferent clothing and heads to, say, a Home Depot, there to run into the handsome widow his imagination has assured him he'd like to know a little better. Awkwardly aware of his seedy appearance, he mumbles a feeble greeting, exchanges some mindless chit-chat, then watches as the lady goes on her way, conscious of her fine legs and knowing the impression he has made had to have been less than favorable. Dammit, he thinks, why didn't I at least shave and put on a clean shirt?

Good grooming is essential for anyone out and about in the world and in contact with people. Nothing turns off others quicker than an unwashed face, a grubby-looking growth of beard, breath that would fell a moose, or body odor that causes eyes to water. And it isn't a matter of just not offending other people; it's a matter of self-esteem, of self-image. The trouble is that for old guys it's easy to convince yourself good grooming no longer matters.

As in much of life, attention to detail is the difference between bringing it off or failing miserably. Thus, almost as bad as not shaving at all is doing a haphazard job in which some patches of whiskers are left unshaven. Or, while attention may be paid to the shave, left untrimmed are the hairs growing in one's ears or nostrils. I once knew a not very pleasant man, a wealthy one, too, who had such a profuse growth of hair in his nose it was not only off-putting but downright repulsive. Talking with him I found it difficult to look anywhere other than at his nose. Other people who knew him experienced the same compulsion, and he still may be wondering why few of those he encounters seem to have trouble looking him in the eye.

If one is even reasonably alert as a young buck he realizes that among the physical attributes women check out before adding him to her list of possible mates are his hands. I'm not sure exactly what it is they look for, but I'm quite certain heading the checklist are clean, closely trimmed fingernails. Raw, chapped hands with cracked fingers are a no-no, as are warts, or a profusion of hair on the backs of hands. A man needn't have the long, pale and slender fingers of, say, a concert pianist, but his hands have to indicate that he pays some attention to them. He can be a grease monkey whose hands are a mess from clock punch-in to clock punch-out, but a woman will take that into consideration — and favorably, too — if it's obvious that at the end of his working day the guy has done his best to get his hands clean. He can have fingers like clichéd sausages, hands like the equally clichéd hams; it won't matter as long as they're clean and his touch with them is caring and gentle.

Old guys tend to forget these basics, not paying any attention to their hands unless they have a hangnail, a split nail, or a bumper crop of livid liver spots. But the ladies, bless 'em, don't change; they're still checking out your hands, still looking for clean, trimmed fingernails. Men check out each other's hands as well, noting their shape and general condition. To a man whose fingernails are clean as a matter of course, the guy with on-going dirty fingernails is a kind of social pariah.

Right up there on the list of checkpoints, not only by women but also by most people an old guy is apt to meet in the course of getting from one day to the next, is clean, neat-looking hair. Not unusual at all is to hear someone — quite possibly a woman, granted — speak of an old gent as having "a fine head of hair." The reality is that dull, straggly, greasy-looking hair, be it long or short, profuse or thin, is a turn-off. Yet a myth among a number of old guys is that shampooing their hair more often than every three or four days or more increases the pace at which they're losing it. Unless you wash it with battery acid or something equally corrosive, hair loss has nothing to do with frequency of shampooing. In fact, a clean balding scalp is a lot healthier than a sparsely thatched scalp that isn't clean. If you go hatless and are out and about, a certain amount of normal dirt in the air (particulate matter) is going to fall and accumulate on your scalp. If you wear a hat or cap, your scalp is going to perspire, even on frigid days. That in mind, make it a point to have a bottle of shampoo handy whenever you bathe or take a shower. You needn't scour you hair as you would a frying pan; a light shampoo will do, but making certain to get your hair clean is an essential.

After a few generations of being shouted at by radio and television commercials and battered by print advertising, it shouldn't be necessary to point out that having dandruff, or the appearance of having dandruff, is not a social grace. To the contrary, it's a put-off; eyes invariably go to "snow" on one's shoulders. Fortunately, the condition can be if not cured at least controlled through the use of suitably medicated shampoos, any number of which are available over-the-counter (OTC) in drugstores and supermarkets. More stubborn cases should be brought to the attention of a good dermatologist.

Unfortunately, a lot of people, especially men (so it seems), are afflicted with what old, back-of-the-book ads in magazines referred to as "the heartbreak of psoriasis," a chronic scaling skin condition that among other locales can and often does manifest itself on one's scalp. When the hair is combed or brushed the whitish psoriatic scales are loosened and, as is so with dandruff, show up on one's shoulders. Here again there are OTC medicated shampoos claiming to hold psoriasis scaling in check, perhaps even claiming to cure it, but personal experience (mine) has indicated the best hope of coping with the condition is treatment by a competent dermatologist.

No secret to any old guy is that his skin doesn't have the glow or the elasticity and resiliency it once had. As we age our skin tends to become drier and drier, and as it does it sloughs off at an increased rate so that by the time we reach our late sixties we risk being reduced to a little pile of dusty scales. I'm stretching it, of course, but we really do have to pay more than customary attention to our skin, especially our facial skin.

Simply washing and toweling the face removes a certain amount of "dead" skin, and if we shave with a blade even more of it is scraped off by the razor, leaving behind a fresher, more "alive" appearance (to say nothing of what a blade shave does for one's morale). But if we wash and towel and then shave with an electric razor, even if we use a "pre-electric" lotion, most of the remaining "dead" skin stays put, tending to result in a dry, matte-finish look. In either instance — blade or electric — called for is a post-shave moisturizer, and let's have no indignant snorting about moisturizers being for sissies. Moisturizers needn't be perfumed, and there's no need to apply them heavily. A few drops or a dime-sized blob can be briefly rubbed together between the palms, then applied to the face from forehead to neck. The effect is immediate — healthier looking skin that in turn increases your confidence in your appearance, and as a result you'll go out the door on the make for the day.

There is, as the cliché has it, no accounting for taste. Some people have taste, some people do not. You need only watch motion picture industry Oscar night on television to appreciate that money has nothing to do with it. Bad taste in dress is bad taste in dress, even if the bad taste sets its wearer back thousands of dollars. Surely my wife and I aren't the only ones who wonder, upon seeing some supposed glamour queen or the pop-icon-of-the-week show up on Oscar night, "What in the world does she/he have on her/his mind?"

It's a theory of mine that somewhere along in the 1960s people stopped simply getting dressed and instead began donning costumes in order to play roles. They stopped being themselves and instead became imagined characters. Thus, if you rode a motorcycle, you had to "wear colors, man," the grungier the better. If your laissez-faire philosophy coincided with that of the hippies, it was all but *de rigueur* to let your hair grow long and start dressing like one, thus serving notice that you, too, thought in psychedelic terms. Surface became everything; what was inside wasn't important, or was incidental. Just about all of pop culture, from its music to its art to its forms of dress, was intended to shock. The Woodstock Generation let it all hang out, and as we've come to appreciate, it was not a very pretty sight.

An early 19th century Frenchman named Anthelme Brillat-Savarin wrote, "Tell me what you eat, and I will tell you what you are." The same train of thought can be applied to the clothing we wear. Dress like a biker, ergo you're biker, and thus a bad news dude, man. T-shirts started making statements presumably reflecting what their wearers wanted observers to know. Clothing became "vertical;" i.e., intended for a specific purpose. A pair of ordinary shorts, for example, shorts worn to play tennis, softball, ride a bicycle, do a little gardening — whatever — became passé. Instead there evolved special shorts for bicycling (those hideous Spandex thingies), shorts for jogging, shorts in which to work out, shorts for the outback, shorts in which to plant tulip bulbs, multi-pocketed shorts for photographers, and, believe it or not, "fishing shorts." Name an activity, there's a pair of shorts that if not worn doing it broadcasts to one and all that you're just not with it.

This is all nonsense, of course, and it encourages people to wear clothing that in their right mind they wouldn't wear. Not in public, anyway. Who among us hasn't seen pushing her cart in a supermarket a sweat-shirted woman of more than ample behind, just in from the gym and still wearing a pair of those cling-like-glue thigh-length workout shorts? Far from appearing to be "with it," she looks like just another fat ass. But the activity calls for the outfit, and that's what she's determined to wear, ludicrous though it may look on her.

What has been lost here is dignity, and if nothing else I want my fellow old guys to have the dignity their years and experience warrants. I'd like them to be mindful of and appreciate that regardless of the extent to which they've dropped out or abandoned ship, people look to them and at them for a certain reassurance that this approaching calamity known as old age needn't be the crisis, the disaster they fear it might be.

As mentioned earlier, I live in Florida, South Florida, among an ever more bountiful crop of old guys. They're seen everywhere (too often driving a snappy thirty-miles-per-hour in the left lane). The climate being what it is, a lot of these old guys wear knee-length shorts, and if I never again see a pair of black dress socks on a pair of pale, spindly old legs — often with sandals, yet! — it will be too soon. It's another cliché, one of which everyone under the age of fifty makes fun. When I overhear young people sniggering over some old rube's black socks, I want to rush up and tell the guy he's letting the side down. Because he's an old guy and because he lacks taste or just doesn't give a damn, the rest of us old guys are tarred by the same brush. He's a stereotype, and if there's one thing I don't want an old guy to be — especially me — it's a stereotype.

I see old guys wearing clothing that not only is mismatched, but that screams in protest — passé plaid golf slacks with striped golf shirts, for example, or pea green slacks and an bright red-and-white striped polo shirt. I have no idea what frame of mind is called for to don such outrageous combinations, but I suspect it's either "I don't know any better" or "I don't care." If it's the former, seek help from a style-conscious friend, an established haberdasher, someone of whom people say "He dresses nicely." If it's the latter, once again all us old guys are being let down.

Set aside a certain amount of money each year to update your wardrobe. Sure, you like that old sport coat, but it went out with the Hudson Hornet. So did that glen plaid suit. We've all had the experience of showing up at, say, the funeral of an age peer and seeing other age peers in attendance, among them one or two old guys in ill-fitting suits or mis-matched components that have been hanging in their closets for twenty years or more.

If you're uncertain when you buy clothing, stick to the basics — white or light blue shirts, solid dark grey suits, neckties with either modest stripes or small patterns, sun tan slacks, solid color polo shirts, plain, solid dark color socks (no clocks, please), straightforward belts. In a dark blue blazer jacket worn with dark grey slacks, black, well-shined shoes, black socks, and a white or light blue shirt and quiet tie, you're dressed for just about any eventuality — a wedding, funeral, party, dinner for two, even a board meeting.

A good rule of thumb when it comes to buying clothing is to avoid any item of dress, including footwear, hawked in the pages of publications aimed at seniors. The ads all but shout, "Hey there, Gramps, here's something nice and comfy." Such stuff is akin to Romeo slippers and about as dated. People will have no trouble realizing you are an old guy; you needn't dress the part, too.

On the other hand, don't go overboard. Extremes, granted, but absolutely ridiculous in appearance are old guy hippy-types with greasy grey, usually thinning ponytails wearing shirts open to the waist, and hanging from their neck some form of medallion. I can't imagine what they have in mind, perhaps trying to look like Willie Nelson (who to me always looks like he needs a bath), or an aging cloak-and-suiter prowling for chicks on South Beach. Anyway, the look was corny from the start, and it hasn't improved with age. It's another example of a costume, of role-playing, and the act being presented is laughable were it not so sad.

An old guy icon is headgear. Some of the damnedest-looking hats and caps you'll ever see can be found on the heads of old guys. Usually such a hat or cap is a favorite, one the guy has worn for years, and more often than not it looks its age. My personal unfavorites are the pork pie-types — made of some type of fabric, they feature round, flat crowns attached to broad, drooping or wavy brims. Okay for golf or tennis, maybe, for yard work, even fishing or out in a boat, but certainly not for everyday out-and-about wear. I'm also put off by stained, greasy-looking discolored peaked caps, especially those bearing advertising (e.g., "Chew Red Man"). And right up there on my personal list of headgear no-nos are woven-fabric hats and caps sold under the Kongol name; I've never seen anyone look good wearing one, even the late and handsome U.S. Open golf champion Payne Stewart.

The thing about so much old guy headgear is that it's undignified and subjects its wearer to ridicule, even scorn. And if there's a single, overriding message to be found in these pages it's a quest for old guy grace and dignity. We owe it to each other.

3

S-E-X

I once had a terrific boss, a former newspaperman named Ned Benham. We often lunched together, usually at a downtown restaurant in which we'd be all but certain to see at least two or three genuinely attractive women. He was nearing retirement age at the time, but the accumulated years did in no way diminish his powers of or pleasures in observation.

This one day we were privileged to be seated at a table near a spectacular, handsomely turned out creature, prompting Ned, after taking in the package in its entirety, to say, *sotto voce*, "Oh, sweetheart, could I disappoint you."

That in mind, what follows will be brief (reminding me of another Ned Benham insight regarding aging swains — "This won't take a minute, did it?").

As I'm all but certain is true of most old guys, I note occasional newspaper ads touting therapies for impotence, prompting me to wonder what the advertisers know that I don't know. Very often such ads list no names of either medical doctors or psychologists, professionals you'd assume would be among those addressing the issue. When just the somewhat vague name of a "clinic" is given as the advertiser, one is apt to have visions of an exotic harem in which practiced houris somehow manage to raise the dead, or at least try to. More likely, however, is that the ads are aimed at mid-life bucks distracted by problems at home, on the job, or at the office, and I can't for the life of me imagine, short of some form of device or injection, what such therapy might involve.

And of course there's the constant hawking of male potency medications, especially on TV and the Internet. Rarely does a prime time hour go by that some macho-looking guy isn't assuring viewers he takes the stuff. Any computer user's morning check of incoming e-mail includes not only pitches for ED cures (Erectile Dysfunction, no less), but also promises of guaranteed penis enlargement. For old guys, such pitches, the "tele-dudes" notwithstanding, tend to fall on deaf ears, and not necessarily as a result of being resigned to inevitability.

What I've observed is that no one — medical doctor, mind-tinkerer, chemist, tarot-card reader, herbalist, or the like — has addressed what I think may in fact be the way things are with old guys . . . plain and simple loss of interest.

Once it dawns on an old guy that short of buying her an acorn-sized diamond, a Rolls Royce, or a penthouse on the Grand Corniche, a possessor of the form divine isn't about to be any more than polite to him, if that, his interest starts to flag. He comes to realize that in what author Philip Wylie long ago referred to as "a gentleman's ball game of some merit" he no longer is a player. Accordingly, sex tends to fade as a compelling subject, its now and then intrusion on his thoughts confined to reminiscence, or perhaps admiration of the proverbial well-turned ankle, but that's about all. What it boils down to is summed up in what a friend of mine calls an old guy's pot belly — "A monument to a dead dick." That may be a bit harsh, yet no less truthful.

Still, there are among us practicing old roosters and would-be old roosters, and the messes and traps into which this holdover capacity leads them can be both comedic and tragic. Apart from the potential danger of embarrassment, violence and disease, the aging rooster on the prowl may as well sport a forehead tattoo proclaiming him to be fair game. A victim of delusion, he thinks the interested glances he's getting from the sleek-looking package at the other end of the bar is for him as an individual, because he's still attractive, still a deft hand with the ladies. What he really is is a mark, and those "interested glances" translate loosely as "Well, well, what have we here?"

This and similar preludes to disillusionment, regret and chagrin for old guys is played out daily in countless ways ranging from being busted for soliciting a decoy hooker (spelled C-O-P) to spending a half-hour or so with a real one and waking up with watch, wallet, and dignity gone. And such victims aren't always among what society deems the lower classes; the police force in any reasonably populous locale can confirm that "johns" include those from the "right" side of the tracks as well as those less privileged. Even more sad if not tragic is the old widower who after acquiring and wallowing in the ministrations of a seemingly accommodating new roommate returns home one day to find his house or apartment stripped — furniture, dishes, pots, pans, linens, books, clothes . . . all of it gone. Think, too, of the smitten old softie who in what amounts to an exchange for access to remembered delights gives his new ladylove a credit card, maybe even an ATM card and his PIN number. The devastation can be horrendous.

Depressingly sad are old guys who start hanging around "adult" book stores and video shops. To each his own, perhaps, but patronage of this sort is demeaning to all those involved — the buyer and voyeur, the seller, and the pathetic exploited creatures depicted in the proffered porn. What's worse is when old guys bring this crap home where it can be discovered by a wife of forty years, or a daughter or son. Whatever credence they've built up over the years as a husband and a father is instantly dissipated, reducing them to just another horny old goat who should know better.

Placing old guys at similar risk, to say nothing of jeopardizing self-respect, is Internet porn, a particularly vicious manifestation of the genre. I've been told of one old guy, a retired U.S. Army colonel, no less, who during his nightly wee small hours pit stop often detoured to his computer to call up porn. Caught red-handed one night by his wife, ever since he has been sleeping in the guest room and getting his own breakfast.

Wives of long standing, particularly loving and wise wives, are aware of what more often than not happens to men as they age. They know that after its peak when a man is in his early twenties, male sex drive gradually wanes. They appreciate the validity of what Lord Lyttleton, in his 18th century "Advice to a Lady," put forth: "The lover in the husband may be lost." And in truth they, too, even though they may have been enthusiastic slap-and-tickle participants over the years, may find their sex drive isn't as ardent as it once was. Rather than what my late brother referred to inelegantly as "hot fat injections," aging ladies may prefer being held, caressed, cuddled, snuggled up with and to. A cheerful "Good morning" smooch accompanied by an affectionate pat on the rump can help assure a veteran wife of her aging husband's on-going interest and regard.

When it comes to old guys, what film director Alfred Hitchcock called "the McGuffin," or linchpin of the story being told is vanity; they find it difficult to admit to themselves that erections and the subsequent presumed use thereof no longer are applicable to their lives. The expression "cock o' the walk," in fact the etymological leap from cock (rooster) to penis, implies strength, vigor, virility. Surrender of that implication, that image, ingrained in males from infancy and culturally reinforced throughout time, is done so grudgingly, and withdrawal from the field is with great reluctance. Yet withdraw we must.

Sex is with us from cradle to grave, but the interval in our lives when we are active participants in its practices are just that, an interval in our lives. Now, as old guys, that time has passed, and we're into a new and different time in our lives, a time during which scoring with the ladies no longer is a priority. Instead, it is, or should be, a time of both internal and external discovery, a time when we come to appreciate that we can carry on an extended conversation with a woman without there hovering overhead thoughts or implications of sex.

4

Ah, Yes, the Little Woman

Okay, so you're an old guy and there she is, that li'l darlin' with whom you've shared most of your life, your helpmeet, the mother of your children, your best girl, in short, your wife of x-number of years. She's there, going about her daily routines in much the same manner she always has, and here you are, a so-called retiree who no longer has an office or job (spelled R-E-F-U-G-E) to go to, a clock to punch, a post-working-hours ginmill in which to rub elbows with your peers. If you were to consult most women in such a situation, and assuming they spoke the truth, I'm reasonably certain they'd tell you having their husbands underfoot day and night is driving them nuts.

Veritable folk lore, especially in so-called retirement communities, are tales of retirees and their wives in a typical supermarket. Pushing the cart as she browses the shelves, he wants to know what she's buying and why. He tells her, at last, that he never has liked Belgian endive, or acorn squash, or cinnamon-flavored waffles. She reaches for a certain brand of dishwasher detergent, the brand she has used since they first had a dishwasher, the dishwasher that contributed immeasurably to their subsequent domestic harmony, and he's quick to point out that the house brand of dishwasher detergent is eighty-five cents cheaper. She sees a spatula she likes the looks of, and he tells her she already has a spatula and asks why she needs a new one.

There's an army of aging wives out there ready to assure you this sort of itch in their lives is a constant. They wish Harry would busy himself re-reading "Two Years before the Mast," or watching endless re-runs of "M*A*S*H."

Almost as annoying as the would-be artful shopper is the would-be helper, the old guy who wants to help with, say, the housework, but who either takes forever to do what his wife deems the simplest of chores, or, brimming with self-satisfaction, does a slapdash job she has to do over again.

This sort of thing — interfering in the household shopping routine, the "idle hands" compulsion to help with the housework, taking exception to and correcting the wife's methods of performing the routines that for decades have marked her life — is a recipe not only for discontent, but in some instances for in-your-face hostility. This is especially treacherous ground for an old guy who once held a position in which he held sway over others. He was a boss then and he sees himself as a boss now, finding it hard to adjust to any role less than a supervisory one.

The first step toward old guy liberation, then, is to recognize that insofar as your wife is concerned you may well have become a nuisance, and if you don't get out of her hair and out from underfoot she's apt to have at you with a frying pan.

Essential to success as an old guy is having something to do, something to which time and enthusiasm — especially enthusiasm — can be devoted. It can take any number of forms, but a job, even a part-time job, is certain to provide at least some of the psychic income all of us require if we're to feel it worth getting out of bed each morning.

Some years ago in Watch Hill, Rhode Island, I happened in the shop of a builder of boats. It was a small shop in which were made locally-known and appreciated dinghies, rowboats, and on occasion even a Cape Cod catboat. Working on a boat-in-progress on the day of my visit — sandpapering its flanks, actually — was a man who appeared to be in his late sixties, early seventies. I wasn't introduced to him, but later I was told he was the retired president of a bank, and that he showed up every working day for which he was paid an hourly wage, punching a clock in and out. It turned out that all his life he'd wanted to try his hand at building a boat, but for one or more reasons never quite got around to it. Retirement had opened a new door through which he was happy to run, not walk.

Much later, when I began to think about becoming an old guy myself, I remembered that man and admired the choice I assumed he had made. Surely, as a lifelong banker, it was doubtful he needed the job to pay the rent and groceries, so he was working in that boat-building shop because he wanted to work there, wanted to have something to do, a place to go.

With the exception of his youthful apprenticeship, all his working life my father was a supervisor of men, a man who held responsible positions, a man who dreaded retirement as one would dread the plague. Two weeks into mandated retirement he went out the door one morning and by late afternoon returned home with a lunch bucket under his arm. He informed my startled mother that he'd found a job as the timekeeper on a construction project. The pay wasn't much, but that wasn't the point, which was that he was gainfully employed, was still in the game, someone who rolled out of bed each weekday morning with something to do, somewhere to go, people to see, papers to shuffle. The timekeeping job was succeeded by appointment as supervisor of the highway department of the town in which he lived, a job he held until the day he died.

Of course there are old guys who withdraw from the field and retreat to basement workshops, there to crank out book shelves, end tables, wine racks, bird houses, that extra shelf Bertha always wanted in the pantry, and so on. The trouble here is that it soon palls; Bertha runs out of room for all the stuff you're turning out, or friends and neighbors start saying "Thanks but no thanks," and you get to a point where you're no longer in thrall to a new router or a new lathe. Further, this is all out-go, no income. It produces no money, not even a modest amount of money, and thus becomes a hobby, and hobbies, however intriguing they might be initially, in time tend to wear out their welcome. Sure, you can try to sell the stuff you make at crafts shows and flea markets, but soon you come to realize that what you think your time, labor, and materials are worth isn't what those you'd like to be your customers think they're worth. There has to be a better, a more fulfilling way, and there is.

For example, why not take your woodworking skills and get a job, even a part-time job, in a cabinet maker's shop, or get into the business of designing and making custom shelving or cabinetry for boats and recreational vehicles? Making birdhouses you sell $7.50 at a flea market isn't very challenging intellectually. Surely it can't hold a candle to solving some boater's gear storage problem for a couple of hundred bucks plus the cost of the materials. Come home to Bertha with a $200 check in your hand and you're back in the game, once again a player whose time is worth something reasonably substantial.

Another retreat for old guys is an enthusiasm for old cars, often cars they owned as young bucks. Before long following retirement a '56 Olds convertible is being restored in the garage, and the guy has terminal dirty fingernails. Then it's on to Antique and Specialty Car shows, shows that involve travel, "Look-but-don't-touch" anxiety, and, often, the consumption of really bad fairgrounds food. The trouble here is that after about the third show at which

Bertha has spent eight hours on a folding canvas chair, her enthusiasm for old cars and their fans tends to wane; she begins to think maybe her old guy is just a bit out of focus. About the tenth such show she opts to stay home and starts hoping that sometime soon someone will make a godfather offer for the '56 Olds convertible. The trouble here, though, is that the '56 Olds is apt to be replaced by a '68 big block Chevelle, triggering a repeat of the cycle.

What might be more rewarding is to offer such car expertise and enthusiasm to a professional restoration shop or an auto detailing shop. Presumably there's no real pressing need to make money, so you can offer to work for a couple of bucks above minimum wage, even for less. I once knew a retired corporate executive, a car nut with a handsome paid-for house in a fancy part of town, who at age seventy-four was delivering auto parts for $5.50 an hour, uniform and all. His wife thought it was wonderful (he had something to do), and he felt plugged-in, felt that he was in at least a form of action, that he was doing something worthwhile.

Anyhow . . .

The point in all this is the need to appreciate that while age and its consequent retirement may have upended your life, the life of your wife goes on about as before, which is to say she'll continue baking a cherry pie in much the same manner and with the same ingredients with which she always has baked a cherry pie. *You're* the one who has to make the adjustment. It's unfair, to say nothing of unworkable, to shift to your wife the burden of your being. Again, assuming that over the years the two of you have had a rewarding relationship in which each partner has upheld his and her end of the marriage bargain, you can't expect her life to change as radically as retirement has changed or will change your life. You're the leopard who must change his spots, and the best way, probably the only way to do that is by using your imagination.

5

LOSS OF SPOUSE

Before going on, let's get this out of the way.

Assuming you genuinely care for the lady with whom you share the premises, especially one with whom you've lived for decades, one who if you have a child or children is their mother, her death is going to buckle your knees, even if losing her follows a drawn out but ultimately fatal illness you've known all along was certain to culminate in her death. You may think that at such a time you're supposed to be a veritable rock — strong, silent, manly, the sort who brushes aside a few tears and makes certain the rest of the family is bearing up and that post-memorial service guests are getting enough to eat and drink.

Horse hockey!

Don't make a spectacle of it, obviously, but forget any preconceived admonitions against showing your emotions. If you feel you want to, or feel the need to, let the tears flow, the sobs come out. If you've had even a reasonably good marriage you're bound to feel bereft, bound to feel that somehow you've been violated. Invariably, and in addition to feeling the pangs of real sorrow, deaths in my family have made me angry. When, for example, my father died I was outraged. When I lost my only daughter in an automobile accident my overriding emotion was fury:

How dare she be taken away!

Anger at death is healthy, and all the supposedly soothing expressions of sympathy and understanding offered by family and friends will do nothing to bank its fires. For one thing, anger at death is truthful, and for another it reaffirms something that if we're reasonably bright we've come to acknowledge — that from the moment of birth life is a crapshoot, and that for most of us the dice are loaded, and not in our favor. Although referring to the death of oneself, poet Dylan Thomas gave us an all-purpose prescription to deal with it: "Rage, rage against the dying of the light."

If on the other hand your wife's death marks the end of what long has been a sour, perhaps rocky, even debilitating relationship from which you've often wished you could escape — especially a marriage held together "for the sake of the children" — admit it. Face up to it. Don't be a hypocrite and shed crocodile tears, again "for the sake of the children," or to "keep up appearances." You can't fake that sort of thing, and if you try to you're going to be exposed for what, in such circumstances, you are — a fraud. You needn't broadcast it, of course, but if the death of a barely bearable wife results in a sense of relief, of freedom, don't feel obligated to go into a song and dance of ersatz sorrow. The death of a virago spells relief not only for the left-behind husband, but also for the circle of immediate friends and acquaintances, even an entire community.

An old guy I once knew who for years had felt himself trapped in a loveless marriage that owed its existence to habit more than to anything else showed up on the first tee three days after the death of his wife. When the guys in his regular foursome tried to express condolences he cut them off. "Look, fellas," he said, "let's not discuss it. She's gone, and that's that." Then, looking from face to face as he waggled his driver, he said, "The usual bet?"

Regardless of whether your marriage to the departed has been sweet or sour, fair or foul, a blessing or a burden, and regardless of how you feel about and react to her death, you should be aware there are a small army of . . . well, parasites anxious to exploit your loss, especially if you are deep in grief. If you allow them to, certain undertakers and/or so-called funeral directors will cheerfully run up a tab of multiple thousands of dollars, a tab they're not a bit hesitant to hire a battalion of lawyers to collect. All the while they'll be unctuous about it, fairly oozing understanding and sympathy, yet with one goal uppermost in their minds — separating from you as much of your cash as possible.

Often they're aided and abetted in this shameful enterprise by the clergy, all of whom stand ready to make the necessary arrangements to assure your loved one's certain passage into a beatific hereafter. Yeah, sure.

Before we go any further I should tell you I'm not a

believer in a deity. I am a man of faith, but not in any form of religion. My faith is in myself, in a few people I know and knew, and, overall, in human capabilities and spunk. As for churches, synagogues, mosques . . . whatever . . . and their priests and administrators, regardless of stripe, I think old Tom Edison had it right when he said "Religion is bunk." I don't believe in a hereafter, don't believe in ghosts, but do believe that what is referred to as one's soul, whatever that may or may not be, ceases to exist when the living body in which it is contained dies.

I'm all for avoiding what writer Jessica Mitford years ago entitled her best-selling book — "The American Way of Death." We tend to make a big and expensive production out of what should be a simple and natural process dictated principally by concerns for public health; i.e., the digging of a hole in the ground and the burial therein of the deceased. Other and perhaps more primitive (or enlightened) societies have had different ways of reaching the same end. For example, certain native Americans disposed of their dead by immolating them in funeral pyres, and we're told that in Eskimo society it once was the practice to place the dying on sleds, strap them down and take them far out on the ice, leaving them there to freeze to death.

Starting perhaps with the ancient Egyptians, probably even earlier, it was only with the evolution of religion as out-and-out theater that the aftermath of death became a

Hollywood production. One need only recall photographs of bodies stacked in Bosnia, or of the mass graves in Iraq to appreciate that the ministrations of undertakers and the benedictions of clergy have nothing to do with death, or with passage to a mythical hereafter. Dead is dead, leaving behind only a carcass and memories, and a $500 "no service" cremation is all that's required, both by law and by your own sense of having fulfilled your obligations.

A writer friend once had mounted on a wall in the kitchen of his home a bulletin board which served as a sort of family clearing house. On it was kept a big calendar as well as notes calling attention to the dates of his kids' school events, doctor and dentist appointments, upcoming birthdays, trip dates, vacations . . . whatever. Also pinned on it was a life insurance company ad clipped from a magazine. The ad's photo illustration showed a number of bills fanned out on a desktop, its overline in large type reading, "Who would take care of these if you weren't here?" Across the face of the ad in bold red grease pencil my friend had scrawled, "Who cares?"

Spang-on, says I. Surely the deceased couldn't care less. Funerals, then, are for the living, who should know better than to underwrite such nonsense. By all means, should you be so inclined, have some sort of memorial for your dear departed. But make certain the post-service bar is well stocked. If for some reason you and the departed hadn't agreed previously to a "rock bottom" cremation, and dear Mildred told you she wanted a funeral worthy of direction by Cecil B. DeMille, she's beyond knowing or caring that you've had her remains cremated and her ashes scattered in a favored glen, on a certain body of water, or in that deep bunker to right of the green on No. 7, the bunker from which she never was able to extricate herself short of tossing out her ball. If a child or the children object, saying, "But you promised Mother," tell them the decision was whether to spend money on an elaborate funeral or leave it to them in your will. If they still fail to see the light, tell them to grow up.

If your in-laws express their displeasure at your seeming insensitivity, even blasphemy, tell them what was done was between you and your late wife, and that they should butt out because it's none of their damn business.

This all may sound like so much cynicism, that I must be a cold, unfeeling s.o.b. Not so. It just is that to be a successful, by which I mean a *contributing* old guy — i.e., someone who still retains within the desire and the ability to give service and pleasure to others, and thus experience an on-going sense of self-worth — you have to divest yourself of excess baggage. All the grieving in the world isn't going to bring Mildred back, so let up on yourself.

A long-gone writer named Jerry Root once observed that men are a collective lode of guilt, and that women spend their entire lives mining that lode. Realize in your bones, then, that Mildred has left the building. Remember her of course, but don't mourn her forever. She won't know it if you do, and no one else will care. Constant mourners, most of whom, truth be told, just feel sorry for themselves ("Who'll make dinner?" "Who'll do the laundry?"), are a pain in the ass to everyone who knows or comes in contact with them.

Losing your wife is a chapter in your life, a chapter that now is concluded. Turn the page, then, and get on with it.

6

MONEY, MONEY, MONEY

There are few things in the course of getting from one day to the next that command more attention then our finances, and unless you're a former big shaker with so much in reserve you figure to die before you run out, money and the need for or lack thereof is a constant in your life.

Unfortunately, not only is it a constant, it's a means, perhaps even the means by which our status in society is measured. Are we keeping up with the Joneses, and are our peers aware that we're keeping up with the Joneses? The rub here for an old guy is that unless you know beforehand that you have the means to comfortably keep pace with the Joneses, you'd do well to sit down with a calculator, a pencil and a sheet of paper and do a lot of hard-nosed thinking and figuring. Straining to "keep up appearances" is a known cause of insomnia, to say nothing of gastric distress.

Let's assume you receive Social Security plus a modest pension, and maybe have a little something coming in from some stock, a CD (Certificate of Deposit), or property you own, all together enough to enable you to keep the house (providing ever-rising taxes don't put you out on the street) or pay rent, keep food on the table, clothes on your back as well as on the back of the lady with whom you share the premises, and that you own a fairly new paid-for car in which you can afford to put gasoline. Let's say, too, there's something left over for the extras that add to the zest of living — occasional travel, gifts for the family at Christmas, attendance at an occasional ball game, a movie or theater outing, dinner once a week or so in a good restaurant, a bottle of decent wine every now and then, perhaps club membership of one type or another, even a vacation during which, while you can't afford to be the last of the big time spenders, you don't have to go "on the cheap."

Let's assume further that before marrying you your wife worked and therefore receives Social Security, not a big check, perhaps, but certainly nothing to sneeze at. This being so, a lot of potential friction can be avoided by having it understood her check goes into the common pot. If you're handling the household accounts, make sure the lady has whatever she needs — new clothes, the occasional bauble, sessions at the hair dresser, manicures, pedicures, now and then indulgences of the grandchildren, and so on (an exception might be so-called cosmetic surgery around her eyes she assures you will make her look years younger; it doesn't, just somewhat different), but also agree the two of you are in this thing together and that your funds in common are to be dispersed on the basis of what's of benefit to and appropriate for the two-partner firm you've established.

Now when you've figured all this stuff up — the income and the out-go — and experience a slight sinking feeling at the pit of your stomach, it's time to, as they say, re-think the priorities. You may have to face the fact the Joneses will just have to go on without you, meaning you may have to resign from the club, cancel the magazine subscriptions, book two weeks in Florida rather than a month, cancel the lawn service, do away with or reduce your donations to charity . . . whatever. The plain fact is you have to cut back, have to make some changes, have to adjust your new life as an old guy to be consistent with the changed financial circumstances in which you now find yourself.

What can't be stressed enough here is that there's no stigma attached to the need to do so. Resigning from the club because you no longer can afford your membership is no disgrace, nor does it detract from your worth as a human being. Far worse, it seems to me, would be to struggle to "keep up appearances," a struggle that eventually you're certain to lose and thus made to feel and look foolish.

For peace of mind, hold onto as much of your pre-old guy life as seems advisable and/or desirable, but don't hesitate to make adjustments that in turn will make more palatable and less stressful your new life as an old guy. Who knows, by chucking old "priorities" you may find a new and exhilarating freedom.

One thing that should be paramount in your mind at all times is an awareness that your old guy status marks you as prey for a host of charlatans and pirates eager to plunder your bank account, in effect to steal your life. So true for an old guy is the hoary adage, "If it's too good to be true, it's too good to be true," or as the eminent philosopher Sugar Ray Robinson once put it, "Ain't nobody give you somethin' for nothin'."

Rarely does a day go by that a newspaper doesn't report on some poor old soul being taken for every dime he or she is worth. The cons by which such outrages take place are too numerous to list and describe, but in general you should be skeptical of "good deals," of "once in a lifetime" opportunities, of telephone calls from slicksters assuring you you've won "an all-expenses-paid Caribbean cruise for two."

Keep in mind that poor old yokel who spent every dime he had flying to Tampa to claim the cash prize a promotional letter from a magazine distribution outfit had advised him he'd won. You needn't be super-sophisticated to appreciate that any widely ballyhooed promise of large scoops of cash is sucker bait. I shake my head in wonderment that people, usually oldsters, still get taken in by swindles as old as time.

In a Damon Runyon short story entitled "The Idyll of Miss Sarah Brown," a gambler son is cautioned by his gambler father:

"Son, no matter how far you travel, or how smart you get, always remember this: Some day somewhere a guy is going to come to you and show you a nice brand-new deck of cards on which the seal is never broken, and this guy is going to offer to bet you that the jack of spades will jump out of this deck and squirt cider in your ear. But, son, do not bet him, for as sure as you do you are going to get an earful of cider."

What we're advocating here is an even keener eye on the seeming kindness of strangers. Loveable you may be, but remember that as an old guy you're fair game, and not just for out-and-out cons; there are some legitimate and quasi-legitimate schmoozers out there as well.

For example, mentioned earlier were the undertakers and funeral directors who feast on human sadness and misery. Add to your "keep-a-sharp-eye-on" list stock brokers, investment counselors, health care quacks (no, even though eager to administer a series of so-called treatments, chiropractors cannot cure most of what ails you, nor can ground up apricot pits cure cancer), shady lawyers, car sales personnel (no, that genial car salesman oozing sincerity is not your friend), cemetery plot salesmen, home improvement contractors and repairmen, agents eager to sell you unnecessary insurance, auto mechanics, TV repairmen, roofing salesmen, mobile work crews who claim to refinish driveways . . . in short just about anyone who charges fees, works on commission, or demands up-front money. Too often the fees charged are pulled out of a hat (in other words, whatever the traffic will bear), and sales tend to be pursued for the sake of the commission to be earned rather than the welfare of the buyer. Up front "good faith" money usually is money you can kiss goodbye. There are exceptions, of course, but before you crack open your wallet, make certain you know what you're doing and with whom you're dealing. Talk to friends, call the local Better Business Bureau, maybe even check with your local police.

If you're a widower, beware, too, of handsome or semi-handsome and somewhat younger women who seem eager to take you under their all-encompassing, semi-motherly wing. These ladies operate with distressing success on the premise "There's no fool like an old fool." In return for a few home-cooked meals and a little implied but rarely delivered slap-and-tickle, they've left many an old guy in what sociologists refer to as "reduced circumstances."

I don't claim to be any kind of financial advisor, and in fact am rather ignorant of stock markets and how they operate. I know nothing of bonds, annuities, debentures, treasury bills, 401(k)s and the like, so I can't advise you, as an old guy, what to do with your money. What I do understand are savings accounts and certificates of deposit, both of which are like the proverbial tortoise in the race with the hare — slow but sure. The only real estate in which I have an interest is my own house and the lot upon which it sits. On the other hand, I don't owe a dime to anyone, and I sleep very well, thank you. My gratitude for this peaceful state of mind was given added significance in the wake of the post-9/11 stock market collapse; friends of mine took a bath, often finding themselves in a real financial bind, especially when faced with the soaring costs of health care. Some lost weight and some are still losing sleep.

To paraphrase an old saw, when it comes to money my eyes are not bigger than my stomach, and yours shouldn't be either. Stick with what you know, and regardless of how enticing someone may make a deal sound, don't jump off, or allow yourself to be pushed off, the ends of any financial docks.

Here's something else to consider: These days, in a number of households (mine being one), a family's money is handled by the wife, and if she dies the left-behind widower often hasn't a clue not only as to the whereabouts of the family checkbook but also the name and location of the bank or banks in which the family funds are deposited. If this describes your situation, make certain you know "where all the bodies are buried." Know where she keeps any stock certificates and any bonds she may have bought, even deeds to real estate. There have been instances whereby a widower didn't find out until his wife died that over the years she had, in one way or another, squirreled away a small fortune. Further, there have been instances in which the husband never finds out, which explains in part the *raison d'etre* for people who make a living tracking down missing heirs.

The same "not a clue" situations apply to widows, of course, but in these pages, as I hope you've noticed, the concern is for old guys.

Finally, paste this one in your hat: "Your dollar is your best friend." That was an often repeated maxim of my late mother-in-law. She was the most generous of souls to her family and to those in need, but she never lost sight of the absolute necessity to remain afloat, and neither should you.

7

TO YOUR HEALTH

This may take awhile; there's a lot to cover.

Up front, let me assure you you're not in as bad a shape as you think you are or might be. Old guys are subject to a number of ills, true, but more than a few of them are self-induced, or if not self-induced self-prolonged.

One reaction to becoming an old guy is to seek sympathy. The hard fact of old age is so offensive, so insulting, the instinctive reaction to it is to want a motherly society to pat your head and say "Poor lad, poor lad, too bad you had to get old."

In lieu of the head-patting and the empathy we're unlikely to receive we tend to try making certain we're deserving of society's attention; we want those around us to appreciate the calamity that has befallen us. Accordingly and perhaps unconsciously we start to experience lower back pains, shoulder aches, knees begin to hurt, fingers to stiffen. The word "arthritis" enters our vocabulary with increased regularity. We start paying more than passing attention to display ads and TV commercials hawking nostrums promising "pain-free nights" and "all-day relief." In this new and somewhat debilitating state nothing becomes more rewarding than to have a family member or friend express or demonstrate sympathy — a "How're you feeling this morning, Dad?," or a brief and caring back rub, an extended helping hand, can make your day in that any solicitation addressed to what ails you reaffirms your significance, your role in the lives of others.

Listen to your peers talk with each other and you'll be impressed (and depressed!) by the frequency with which aches, pains, and illnesses in one form or another are discussed. It takes no special ability to detect in the voices you'll overhear the notes of semi-pride and self-satisfaction in the words, "I have a three o'clock doctor's appointment Tuesday." What's being said, really, is, "See? I'm of such significance that on Tuesday afternoon the attentions of the entire medical establishment will be focused on me. That should demonstrate to you how important I am." This sort of thing is, of course, a spin on the old "Let me tell you about my operation" gag; it seeks the attention and the sympathy of others.

Don't misunderstand what's being put forth here. Like any mechanism, the human machine eventually starts to show evidence of wear and tear, some of the symptoms thereof not unlike those mentioned above. That in mind, don't be surprised by their advent, and don't panic when they're first experienced. The process is normal, or as my "health care provider," a no-nonsense man in whom I have absolute confidence, once said to me, "What you're suffering from is youth deficiency."

In truth many of the inevitable physical woes that

beset old guys can be addressed and alleviated, at least somewhat, by swallowing (with water, please) a couple of aspirin tablets. You can, of course, opt for one of the more expensive over-the-counter (OTC) pain-killers, or what are billed as pain-killers, but their effectiveness over plain old aspirin is marginal at best.

If you can stand the "heat" it generates, I've found the application of any preparation containing capsicum will alleviate certain types of pain — aching joints, stiffness, and the like, even headaches. I suspect it's effective because the burning sensation generated by the capsicum tends to divert your attention from the pain from which originally you sought relief. Be careful of this one, however, because it can "burn" your skin. Over the years capsicum preparations have worked for me, possibly because I've got skin like a rhino.

I've also found that so-called sports creams can provide temporary (very) relief of the above-mentioned woes, but some of them are messy to apply, feel icky on your skin, and smell like a locker room rubbing table.

A change in diet can work wonders as well. If, for example, you're wild about *tamales* and seem to be experiencing heartburn every time you shovel 'em down, all the purple pills in the world aren't going to be of much help in relieving your distress. Stop eating tamales, period. On one occasion or another all of us have heard a peer say, placing one hand on his stomach and the other over his mouth as he burps, "Damn, every time I eat stuffed peppers (or whatever) I get gas." How many times does he have to be hit over the head to stop eating stuffed peppers?

If a blood test indicates your cholesterol is too high, stop eating foods high in cholesterol; after all, you can read a product label as well as anyone. Too, down a couple of garlic pills each morning and learn to love oatmeal in all its forms. The usual prescription for having excessive amounts of plug-o in your circulatory system — cholesterol-lowering drugs called statins — not only will enlist you in a regimen that like all drug-taking regimens is best avoided, but also is very apt to bind you up tighter than the proverbial drum, a situation in which you'll either be forced on a parallel regimen of habit-forming laxatives, or will find yourself downing prune juice by the quart while wearing around your neck a feed bag of all-bran cereal.

Morning stiffness of joints, shoulders and lower back are old guy constants. An old guy with whom I played golf a few times, a man then in his mid-seventies, used to say, "If after I get out of bed in the morning I can't stand upright within five minutes, I know it's going to be a bad day." When it was suggested he buy a new and somewhat firmer mattress and sleep with a pillow under his knees, the severity of his lower back pains subsided considerably. In the same vein, early morning shoulder pains often are the result of an awkward, on-your-side sleeping position.

Try falling asleep while on your back, knees propped up somewhat by a pillow. You may well snore loud enough to wake the dead, but chances are your shoulder pains will be considerably eased. I've found that bedside reading until my eyes start to droop allows me to drop off to sleep on my back within only a minute or two of turning out the night stand light. I don't know whether or not the practice is good for my eyesight, but rarely, and then only when stressed, do I toss and turn.

Unavoidable as an old guy (or so I've discovered personally, and have checked with a number of other old guys) is the need to get out of bed to go to the spring at least once every night. Age reduces the elasticity of one's bladder, and sure, there's a prescription drug that may enable you to retain urine throughout your normal period of sleep. But it, too, is a crutch and once again enlists you in a pill-taking regimen. Better is to accept the need to get up and go, the only viable alternative being the use of a bedside hospital urinal, known euphemistically as a duck, a practice certain to offend all but the most understanding and tolerant of female sleeping companions.

As an old guy you can't pay too much attention to your feet, perhaps for the first time in your life, really, and especially if you're a "late in life" or "old age" (e.g., Type II) diabetic supposedly controlling the diabetes through "diet and exercise" as opposed to ingesting some form of drug. You may never have thought of it in such terms, but your feet need exercise, and not just the act of walking. Toes need to be wriggled, arches both extended and curled, ankles rotated. Whenever feasible, go barefoot. If it's too cold to go barefoot, even indoors, wear a pair of those soft moccasin "socks," the point being to allow your feet maximum flexibility.

Make certain your footwear really fits your feet. Most of us have one foot ever so much larger than the other foot, meaning, say, a shoe will fit the left foot perfectly, but its mate will be a bit snug on the right foot. Take your time when you buy shoes. Be picky, and make certain both of them feel comfortable and really fit your feet, realizing that one manufacturer's size 10-C may be fractionally larger or smaller than another manufacturer's 10-C, especially footwear imported from the Far East. Yes, you can buy shoes (any footwear, for that matter) out of a mail order catalog, but be prepared to go to the bother of sending them back if they don't fit perfectly.

Remember as a kid trying to pick up objects — a marble, perhaps, or a pencil, a small stone on a beach . . . whatever — with you toes? If you do, now as an old guy is the time to reprise the act. Your feet will benefit greatly and you'll be rewarded greatly by regular such exercise. You'll retain feeling, increase flexibility, and above all aid the most important aspect of overall foot health, namely circulation.

The keys to achieving and maintaining trouble-free feet are exercise, dryness, warmth, and — vital — cleanliness. And if you have bunions, corns, hammer toes and other such foot ills, invest in having them removed or remedied. The payoff is well worth the expense.

Do all you can to maintain, even increase overall flexibility. To me, the ideal means of doing so is swimming. In fact, any time you can spend in water deep enough to "float" some of the weight off your frame and its joints is beneficial. If you can't swim a stroke, just walking in water at least up to your waist will give you a good workout that won't leave you gasping for breath. Also beneficial are in-water calisthenics — arm and leg exercises, back bends, torso twists, and so on. What it is, really, is a form of hydrotherapy without the tub.

The catch here, of course, is access to water in which you can do all this. Seaside beaches, or inland lakes or ponds, even the old swimming hole, assuming they're safe and aren't polluted, can serve the purpose. In most communities that aren't out-and-out Podunks there figures to be at least one public-access swimming pool, perhaps in a municipal park, recreation area, and so on. During the "off" season (i.e., other than summer) public-access pools are apt to be in a "Y," a high school or college, a hospital . . . whatever. You have to ask around. Such may be open to the public only one day or night per week, but even once a week is better than no pool at all. The point is, find one and take advantage of it. You may feel a little awkward at first, especially if no one is likely to mistake you for Adonis, but get over it; you're not in a pool to be admired, to entertain just by your presence.

If you simply can't get in water of some sort, or just don't care to, make sure you at least stretch, something many of us do instinctively upon awakening. I don't believe in hopping out of bed and immediately running through a series of calisthenics accompanied by deep-breathing exercises. But even before getting out of bed I'm a firm believer in stretching my arms overhead as far as they'll go, in extending my legs straight out and pointing my toes as if reaching to touch bottom. The old Charles Atlas ads that once appeared in the backs of magazines hawked something called "dynamic tension," and in part that's what stretching is — making muscles work with and against each other. You may still be a 125-pound weakling, but at least you'll be a reasonably flexible 125-pound weakling.

The trouble with exercise in any form (or so I've found) is that it's boring. If you have any imagination at all, at some point in an excise regimen, however mild, you're going to feel like a damned fool. You'll ask yourself, "What the hell am I doing this for? Who cares?" Well, you care or you wouldn't be going through the motions. You have to keep in mind the ultimate goal, which is to be a *successful* old guy, an old guy still in the game, still plugged in, and as such it's to your advantage to be able to move about as gracefully as possible. Besides, you'll hurt a lot less.

8

ACCESSORIES AND OPTIONS

Assuming you haven't experienced it earlier in life, something that often goes along with becoming an old guy is thinning hair, and that's okay. Don't sweat it; the process is natural, and it's doubtful anything, despite what someone peddling something may tell you, can slow it down, let alone halt it.

Earlier we mentioned the many charlatans who lick their chops over the prospect of having at an old guy, and among them are those who feast on baldness, or incipient baldness. What must be billions of dollars are spent each year in this country on various forms of hair wishful thinking and rejuvenation, everything from surgically implanted plugs to hair-growing (fuzz-producing?) drugs. There are hair weavers, hair dyes, preparations that color scalp bare spots in simulation of hair, and of course toupees, or, more delicately, hairpieces.

The only guys I've ever seen who could get away with wearing a hairpiece included Bing Crosby and TV weatherman/pitchman Willard Scott (who gave it up, you may recall). Even Frank Sinatra, for all his money, meaning he presumably could afford the very best the toupee trade had to offer, when he got older looked like a guy wearing a rug. A few years back Phil Neikro, the old

Atlanta Braves knuckleballer, managed a women's "major league" baseball team. By that time he had become bald, but because as manager of the team he was going to be in the public eye he deemed it necessary (I assume) to wear a toupee. He must have procured it from the bottom of a circus clown's trunk, for when he was wearing it and you looked at him you'd have trouble keeping a straight face. Instead of adding dignity it made him look ridiculous. And who can forget some of those last public appearances by old Strom Thurmond? His pathetic rug made him look like a character in a burlesque show skit. And how about discredited junk bond flim-flammer Michael Milliken? For all his ill-gotten gains, did you ever in your life see anyone whose toupee appeared more ridiculous? It looked like a hunk of horse hair chair stuffing tacked to his scalp.

I repeat, there's nothing wrong, sinful or illegal about having thinning hair, or with being bald, even if you have yet to reach old guy status. Trying to do something about it is yet another example of allowing ego and vanity to get in the way of innate good sense. Even a guy who has had plug transplants looks like a guy who has had plug transplants. No one is deceived but the patient, and realizing that even he has to feel just the least bit ridiculous. Even more ridiculous is the guy who by "artful" combing seeks to conceal his baldness; his hair parted a half-inch above an ear, or at the back of his head, he then combs — torturously so — or brushes his remaining "fringe" hair over his barren pate, the result appearing not unlike the "hair" on a kewpie doll. For such sad souls, windy days have to be Panic City.

It must be obvious certain bald guys can attract the opposite sex. Their baldness, however, is incidental to their attractiveness. They bring moths to the flame because of their youth and vigor, because of personality, wit, charm, money . . . whatever. Old guys wearing hairpieces remain old guys and aren't about to revel in similar success, possible exceptions being very rich old guys (witness Anna Nicole Whatshername). Instead, they are giggled about, usually discreetly, behind the backs of hands. There isn't a hair piece in the world that can compete with cleanliness, good grooming, good taste, and generosity of spirit.

Another pitfall into which old guys often tumble is the loss of teeth. Not only does losing teeth affect one's enjoyment and ingestion of food, it can alter one's appearance. As a rule of thumb, fight to the very last tooth extraction of your natural teeth. Why? Because there's a certain inner dignity inherent in having one's own teeth, something that somehow reassures us we're still a factor in what comedian Flip Wilson used to call "what's happenin' now." On the other hand, you don't want to be known as "Lone Tooth, the old trapper."

If bridgework of some sort is called for, get a second opinion, maybe even a third opinion. When it comes to such work, dentists and dental technicians can be either skilled artists or ham-handed plumbers. A lady I know, a wealthy lady, at that, went through two or three years of discomfort and constant tinkering at the hands of a klutz who never did get her bridgework right. Finally convinced to seek relief elsewhere, she went to a guy who recognized her problem immediately and had made for her just what was needed, and to the best of my knowledge she has had no trouble since.

Dental implants are tempting, but be forewarned there's a good bit of discomfort involved. They're expensive, too. The cost has to be weighed against the time the work will take, and once they're in place against how long you'll get to have use of them. A former golf pro I knew — a budding old guy — had several dental implants at a cost of thousands of dollars, and within a year or so after the work was completed died. However, implants are functional and cosmetically appealing, and if that's the route you want to go and can go, more power to you.

If all else fails or doesn't apply, dentures may be a necessity, and if they are there are certain rules to heed, the first and most important being don't go on the cheap. Attractive, useful, comfortably fitting dentures cost money, every penny of which is worth spending. For example, upper and lower plates affording orange-y gums and perfectly shaped, evenly spaced whiter-than-white teeth obviously aren't the real thing, and an old guy wearing such teeth can't help but be conscious of them. I mean, he doesn't look like himself and is bound to wonder if others have noticed the change in his appearance. Worse is the new denture-wearer who is conscious of an altered appearance and decides to counter his unease by being be a comedian about his new teeth, making bad jokes about them, or flipping them out in public. Guys like that are oafs and deserve to be crossed off everyone's list.

Attractive, properly fitted dentures are made of superior materials by skilled technicians in modern, out front, well-equipped dental labs. "Going on the cheap" can mean dentures made in some guy's alley garage, or even overseas (e.g., China). All such teeth supposedly are made to a dentist's specifications, and the more skilled and caring the dentist is the more comfortable and attractive the dentures will be. If you've got the right dentist, he or she should be happy to tell you at what lab your dentures are to be made, and it would behoove you to get involved in the process, perhaps even calling and asking to visit the lab.

To give the wearer both comfort and peace of mind, and to fit his or her personality, dentures should be shaped as much as possible like the wearer's natural teeth (exceptions being horribly misshapen or misaligned natural teeth) and colored accordingly. Teeth that have gone a bit off-white with age should be replaced by slightly off-white teeth. Teeth that are somewhat out of line — slightly elevated eye teeth, say, or a slight overbite — can be duplicated as faithfully as possible, something a technician who knows his or her business can do working from a set of a given patient's plaster dental impressions.

The rub is that dedicated attention and the superior materials used in the crafting of quality dentures costs money. Yet the expenditure is worth it if wearing them makes you feel good about yourself. Yes, tap the piggy bank however deeply, and yes, you can cut into the kids' legacy to such an end and not feel the least twinge of conscience. If necessary, you usually can work out some form of "time pay" plan with most denture providers.

On the other hand, if none of the above concerns you and is of no importance, to hell with it. Just be sure any dentures made for you fit comfortably, are kept clean, and that they work, for not much is more bizarre than observing a toothless old guy, his irritating and possibly painful dentures in his pocket, gumming his food, or someone with obviously ill-fitting dentures wrestling with a piece of less than tender steak. What's more, the profile of a toothless old guy isn't likely to launch a thousand ships.

Many years ago I was a reluctant and even then a mildly rebellious Sunday school attendee at the Methodist-Episcopal church in Ardsley, N.Y. Being present when the minister at the time gave a sermon was a howl in that the poor guy's dentures were ill-fitting, and his congregation, especially Sunday school kids dragooned by their parents into also attending the regular service, had trouble keeping straight faces as he *clickety-clacked* his way through his weekly homily. I'm sure the man's salary was a pittance, but a couple of bucks a week of it should have been invested in teeth that fit.

When Arnold Palmer started wearing a hearing aid I became conscious of my age; it was hard to imagine this golfing superman, whose background and childhood was much like my own, as anything less than bulletproof. I mean, not for Arnie the vicissitudes of advancing years. And when he went public with his prostate problems the balloon of my hero worship, while it didn't burst, nonetheless began to leak.

Sitting in New York City's Penn Station one day waiting for a train, I noticed a well-dressed elderly couple being solicitously guided to one of the benches by a uniformed chauffeur carrying identical handsome black leather suitcases. After he sat both the luggage and his presumed employers down, the chauffeur took his leave. The woman then turned to the man and began speaking to him in what sounded to me like rather sharp tones. It was then I noticed the old fellow's hearing aid. This was in the late 1930s or so, and I assume hearing aid technology wasn't very advanced, for its receiver and presumed battery pack consisted of a small black box suspended from a strap around his neck and "worn" on his chest. From the black box a thickish black wire ran up to and was connected to what looked like a small earphone stuck in his ear. Anyhow, when the woman finished what I took to be a rebuke, the old man turned, spoke a few words I couldn't hear, then reached a hand up to the black box resting on his chest and, defiantly and in obvious satisfaction, turned off the juice.

Ever since, whenever I've noted someone wearing a hearing aid I've been reminded of that old man, mindful that his crude apparatus gave him the option of hearing what he wanted to hear and not hearing what he didn't want to hear. And every time I go into a wired public place and am forced to hear some tortured soul screaming out the latest pop music gibberish I think of that old man and his soothing option.

That choice aside, however, these days there's no really valid excuse for someone hard of hearing not wearing a hearing aid. Fitted and adjusted properly, such a device can make a decided difference in one's enjoyment of the people and the events around them. Technological wonders, they're incredibly small in size, and excuses prompted by vanity — they're unsightly, or "make me feel old" — just won't fly. Nor will assertions they're uncomfortable, or too costly. Only half-hearing and not understanding what's said, forever saying "What's that?" or constantly turning up the volume on a radio or a television set negates any thought wearing a hearing aid will make you feel old. Being hard of hearing is a cross to bear, true, but refusing to do anything about it (assuming you can) makes it plain you don't care, not only about your own presence in the scheme of things, but also about what is thought of you.

I've known hard-of-hearing old guys who'll buy a new Buick every few years or so, yet will beg off wearing a hearing aid because "They're too expensive," or "The damn things are a pain in the ass," or "I just can't see myself with this thing in my ear(s)." Baloney! As with good, properly fitted dentures, a good, properly fitted hearing aid is essential and also can be bought "on time."

Unless you're one of the fortunate few, as an old guy or a pending old guy you're probably going to get to learn more about your prostate gland than you care to know. The initial signs of trouble include difficulty in emptying your bladder. Why? Because the prostate is a walnut-sized "doughnut" around the urethra, the piping through which both your urine and your semen passes. As we get older, the prostate gland tends to enlarge, inhibiting the flow of urine from the bladder. In most instances such enlargement can indicate the presence of cancer. Here again we turn to golfer Arnold Palmer.

A few years ago Palmer, himself a prostate cancer victim, made some public interest TV spots urging men, especially older men, to get from their doctor (who, if he's not a urologist, probably will refer you to one) a test called a PSA, which stands for "Prostate Specific Antigen." If the result of the test indicates a PSA of five or six, the doctor may want to go up your, uh, bung with a flexible tube tipped by a small light with which he can check out your prostate, and if it looks suspicious he may reach up there and snip off a tiny piece of tissue upon which a lab will perform a biopsy to determine if cancer is present. The procedure I've described sounds more ominous than it is; there's a little physical discomfort, true, but not much, and the thought of someone going up "the Anal Canal with Gun and Camera" can be, admittedly, somewhat disquieting. But it's worth the imagined indignity, for if ignored, prostate cancer can be a killer.

If the biopsy comes back positive, you have four options:

1. Because prostate cancer is slow to progress, and if you're an old guy who figures to check out in another few years, and if you can get by with restricted urine flow, you can opt to do nothing, just let nature take its course. The danger here, though, is that the cancer can spread . . . fatally.

2. You can opt to have the prostate surgically removed. The rub here is the risk of incontinence and, if you're still a practicing rooster, impotence. The benefits of the surgical approach include the

blissful feeling of satisfactorily emptying your bladder as well as freedom of mind. The Big Bad Wolf is no more.

3. You can undergo radiation treatments, usually every day (except weekends) for up to eight weeks, maybe a little more. Apart from the inconvenience of having to show up five days a week to be zapped, however briefly, there's also the risk of incontinence (so I've been told), and I know of no still-in-the-game old guy who cottons to the idea of being a pissy old man.

4. You can have surgically implanted in your prostate radioactive "seeds" that will zap the cancer on a continuing basis as you go about your daily routine. The advantages of the "seeds" are one-stop service, considerably improved urine flow, and little if any chance of incontinence. You will, however, have what a friend of mine who has had the seeds implanted calls "leakage," by which he means that when you feel the urge to urinate, do so immediately. If you don't, you'll find it impossible to hold back the "leakage" of a few drops, perhaps even a brief spurt, which even though minor nonetheless is detectable as you having pee'd your pants. It's embarrassing,

demeaning, smelly, and clammy. That in mind, until you're certain you can control your bladder and thus avoid leakage, it's a good idea to wear some form of padded, absorbent underwear. Such garments are not unlike briefs as opposed to boxer shorts. They fit comfortably, are not bulky and thus undetectable, and they're available on supermarket and drugstore shelves.

The reason I'm up on all this is that radioactive "seeds" were implanted in my prostate a couple of years ago, and I have first-hand experience of everything about the procedure I've described. The "seeds" also taught me to take to heart some sage advice handed out a few years ago by a slightly older golfing companion, a man who upon heading for the halfway house as we stepped off the ninth green said, "I'll be right with you. Boys our age should never pass up an opportunity to pee."

In the news not long ago was a report of a blood test that obviates the need of a biopsy to detect prostate cancer, so maybe by the time you read this some of the above will be old hat.

Finally, old guys as a group in society are subject to colorectal cancer. You've heard all the noise about its symptoms, mainly the presence of blood in your stools, or rather sudden and somewhat radical changes in bowel habits and performance. Whatever, it's nothing to mess with, and if detected early enough can be cured. A good idea is an annual fecal occult blood sample, the details of which will be explained by your doctor.

9

ABOUT THE MESS

Living where I do, in South Florida, I see a lot of gray hair. Accordingly, much of what I read in the local section of my daily newspaper has to do with the activities, fortunes and misfortunes of so-called seniors, men and women of post-retirement age, most of them anyhow.

Perhaps the saddest such stories are those reporting the lonely death of some poor old soul found to have been living in squalor. Such stories occasionally are reported nationally, a famous case of many years ago being that of New York City's reclusive Collier brothers, two old men, both graduates of Columbia University, who were found to have been living among incredible piles of debris, a notable example being rooms of stacks and stacks of newspapers piled from floor to ceiling.

Just as the old guy who finds himself on his own should learn his way around a kitchen, so too should he learn the fundamentals of keeping a reasonably tidy household. In the motion picture entitled "About Schmidt," the title character, a recent retiree played by actor Jack Nicholson, suddenly loses his wife, and, left on his own, within a short period is shown living in a mess — clothes strewn all over the floor, dirty dishes in the kitchen sink, trash can overflowing, bed unmade, just about all the nightmare things associated with failing to keep ahead of the game. What the depiction of such messiness verifies is that it's not uncommon. In fact, messy digs are legion, the stuff of humor when centered on the apartments of young bachelors and the rooms of teen-age boys (e.g., the comics' "Hi and Lois" son Chip), but the stuff of semi-tragedy when centered on old men living on their own. We laugh at a young man's mess but tsk-tsk at a mess in which an old man is found living.

One of the canards with which boys are raised is that certain household chores are "women's work." It's doubtful a mother ever used the term (unless campaigning against an unapproved of daughter-in-law), the falsehood instead being promulgated by a "macho" father eager to foster a son in the father's image of himself. In truth, other than being in labor prior to giving birth and subsequent breast feeding of the newborn, there isn't much that is exclusively "women's work." Thus the man, young or old, who finds himself on his own and seemingly lost either hires a housekeeper or takes it upon himself to do the dusting and the vacuuming, run the dishwasher, the washer and drier, and whatever scrubbing, scouring and polishing needs to be done. The alternative is chaos that when ignored soon deteriorates to squalor. In turn, apart from being unhealthy, squalor does nothing for the well-being or morale of the individual living in it. An old guy striving to keep about him a shred of grace and dignity is ill-served by chaotic digs.

One key to an orderly life alone is to think small; for example, a studio apartment or a one bedroom condominium as opposed to a two-story, three-bedroom house. The latter can be an albatross. Here's how it too often works:

Bertha dies and Charlie decides to stay put in the house in which they've raised three now-married children. But unless Charlie is a born neatnik, or hires help, or has children who attend to his needs, a house that was big enough for a family of five is soon going to get away from him. First thing you know, an upstairs bedroom is closed off, and because it's closed the heat in it is turned off and it becomes a repository for whatever needs removing from Charlie's sight. In no time at all it becomes an unholy mess, so cluttered Charlie has a hard time even entering it. Then another upstairs bedroom is closed off, and so on until, eventually, Charlie is living in the den off the kitchen, the kitchen itself, and the little downstairs bathroom, all other rooms in the house being closed off and only occasionally entered. He finds himself falling asleep watching television and sleeping through the night in his lounge chair as opposed to opening up and making the den's convertible love seat bed. Sleeps in his clothes, too, and if he withdraws far enough from living among the living he'll start skipping his daily shower, won't even bother to shave, let alone change his clothes. He starts eating cold beans and cold Dinty Moore stew right out of the can. And he starts to smell a little ripe, and then . . . well, you know the drill; one day he keels over and three days later a neighbor who hasn't seen either Charlie or a light in the house calls the cops, and it's another sad story on Page Two of local and state news.

Charlie and the thousands upon thousands like him are simply overwhelmed by the responsibility of housekeeping; they've never done it and have no idea how to go about it. Bertha took care of all that sort of thing; it was his job to be the breadwinner, period. But now there's no Bertha, and dust still accumulates, dirty dishes still pile up, clothes, towels and bed linens still have to be laundered, floors attended to, and if he's to maintain any semblance of order in his life, things still have to be picked up and put away. To neglect any one of these household "chores" is to let the rot set in. Hence the thought to think small, to live in a place the size of which you can handle, especially if you're a rank housekeeping rookie as opposed to a regular Donald Domestic.

I've been told about one old guy who after his wife died sold everything, including his car, and bought himself a small motor home on the theory it presented about all the housekeeping chores he felt he could handle.

There are certain keys to keeping things manageable, one being a schedule you can adhere to, the other being proper housekeeping equipment. The trick to the first is to do a little bit of certain chores every day, to the second determining what needs doing and what you need to do it without making a career out of it.

For example, more than handy is an appliance called an electric broom, a kind of vacuum cleaner in miniature. A few quick passes over wooden and vinyl or ceramic tile floors will eliminate dust balls and anything else one is apt to find on such a floor. If it takes you more than five minutes to "broom" the floor of a bathroom, say, you're not paying attention. Yes, you have to empty them of accumulated dust and stuff and clean their re-useable filters after just about every use, but their convenience and the ease with which they can be zapped around makes them an old guy's housekeeping must. Other items you should have handy include a good straw broom, a squeegee sponge mop, a good vacuum cleaner with a built-in accessory hose and all the attachments (especially a dust brush), a dust rag (an old cotton T-shirt is ideal), a spray can of cleaner/polish (e.g., Endust, Pledge, and the like), a supply of cleaning rags (preferably old hand towels), and a bottle of some sort of cleanser and disinfectant (e.g., Pine Sol). You are now armed to do battle with the monsters of housecleaning.

If you have carpeting or rugs on the floor, make it habit to vacuum every week or 10 days. It shouldn't take too long — a half-hour at the most — and the effect, principally piling that stands even and looks smooth, can be a morale-booster in that you see immediate and pleasing results of your effort. Use the vacuum cleaner's hose accessory and dust brush to dust lamp shades (gently, mind you), picture glass and frames, books, chair arms, legs and crossbars. That done, grab the spray cleaner/polish and the dust rag and have at table tops, the TV set, shelving . . . anywhere dust accumulates. Remove knickknacks, books, coasters, eyeglasses, vases and so on from a table top, say, and give it a quick *pffft* with the spray stuff, then take your dust rag and wipe the surface. The result, painlessly arrived at, will be a clean, shiny, and satisfying surface.

What may at first seem a formidable adversary is the bathroom. For example, being down on your knees in front of a toilet bowl probably isn't what you had in mind. On the other hand, there the damn thing sits, and certainly it has to be cleaned; it's best to not imagine the alternative. So start with the basin and the vanity top. Close the basin's drain and draw it half full of warm water. Add a generous dollop of the liquid or powdered cleanser. In the resultant mixture soak and wring out a piece of old toweling, then wipe the surface of the vanity, the cover of the toilet tank, the medicine cabinet mirror . . . whatever needs wiping. In the process re-dip and wring out your cleaning rag often. Wipe the inside and edges of the basin, paying special attention to the cleaning of its fixtures. Feel the inside surface of the basin with your fingers to make certain you've removed any soap scum. Wring out your cleaning rag as tightly as you can, then give everything a final wipe and drain the basin. Wipe first the fixture and then the inside of the basin with a couple of paper towels and see 'em shine. Again, a morale booster.

If you have a tub, repeat the procedures outlined above; i.e., drain closed, some warm water in the tub, a shot or two of cleanser and your cleaning rag. Make certain to wipe the level surfaces of the tub's edges. If soap scum won't surrender without a fight, take a damp sponge and some powdered cleanser (e.g., Ajax) and have at it. When done, rinse thoroughly. Same thing with a stall shower, but now you'll have to get down on your knees. If you have tile walls around a tub or a stall shower, its grout can be subject to black mildew, so have handy a spray bottle in which you've poured some bleach. A few spritzes of bleach and the mildew is no more.

Now flush the toilet, and when the water in the bowl returns to its proper level dump in a generous shot or portion of cleanser and again get down on your knees. Dip your cleaning rag in the water, wring it out, and wipe clean both sides of the toilet lid and the seat. Re-dip and wring out the rag, then wipe clean the entire outside surface of the bowl. That done, re-dip the rag and without wringing it out wipe up under the lip of the bowl and all around it down to and including the entry to its trap.

And that should do it, the entire process taking no more than a half-hour. Unless you're a real slob, once per week should be about right, and the resultant and lingering smell of the cleanser, especially pine-scented cleanser, serves as an affirmation of a job well done. Who cares? *You* care, or you should.

If you do it yourself, wash small, every-other-day loads of laundry as opposed to mammoth once-a-week loads. If you've never done laundry, be sure to separate dark-colored things from light-colored things, and wash them separately. In other words, don't throw your yard-working or sparkplug-changing jeans in with your dress shirts and the dish towels. If you have a dryer, you'll spare yourself a lot of ironing if you'll remove and immediately fold whatever is in the dryer as soon as the drying cycle ends. Leaving stuff in there on the theory you'll get to it later just adds to the wrinkles.

If doing your laundry yourself isn't in the cards, you can take it to a wash-and-fold laundromat, even to a commercial laundry, the latter, these days, a somewhat pricey proposition.

Ironing . . . ah, yes, ironing. Assuming you never have had to do it, you can learn to iron, the job not being as formidable as it may at first seem. But even if you become adept at it, I'd be lying if I claimed it to be any less tedious. Buy a quality steam iron (before doing so, consult "Consumer Reports," usually available in your local library), and once you've bought one, *read and digest the instructions that come with it!* Make sure you have a sturdy padded surface upon which to use it, wobbly, flimsy ironing boards being a curse and a blight. Start small, handkerchiefs, say, then dishtowels. Gradually you can work your way up from ironing golf shirts, say, to ironing jeans and suntan pants, even dress shirts. You can press dress slacks, too. The progression isn't nearly as time-consuming as you may think, and here again it's best to do a little at a time as you go along rather than facing a discouraging and ticking time bomb pile of stuff that nags to be ironed.

Make your bed each morning, even if all you do is pull the cover up and smooth it out. An unmade bed is a sure sign of an unmade and uncaring mind. Fluff up your pillow, too, a fluffed-up pillow being one of life's rewards. If you bathe or shower at night, say at working day's end, or before or right after you prepare and eat your evening meal, and before you settle down in front of your television set, you'll find your bed a lot more pleasant place in which to sleep in that its sheets and pillow case(s) will remain fresher for a longer period of time (a week's about the limit before a change of sheets and pillow case is called for).

Nothing you do by way of keeping a livable house is more important than uncluttered clothes closets and bureau or chest drawers. What's called for here is a firm dose of realism — toss out or take to Good Will what you don't wear and aren't likely to wear ever again. In my closet as I write this are flannel shirts I haven't worn in ten or more years, a sport jacket I wouldn't be caught dead in, assorted cardigan sweaters I'll never wear, and at least two pairs of shoes that never again will see the light of day, and as soon as I get around to it I'm going to pitch the lot of it out. At least that's what I've been telling myself for the past year or so.

In my chest of drawers I've got enough socks for a small army, some underwear that has lain dormant for years, some initialed linen handkerchiefs I'll never use, sweat pants in which the elastics in the waist and the leg cuffs have given up the ghost, three new golf shirts I'll never wear (still in their original wrappings and given to me as a semi-bribe by a guy who wanted me to write about him in the newspaper for which I worked; besides, I never much liked him), a sweater vest or two that have never warmed anything other than the lower drawer in which they've been housed for at least five years, perhaps even stuff I've forgotten is there.

The point is that I've got to do something about all this stuff. If I die first, my wife will have the chore of pitching it out. None of our sons or grandsons will want it, so I can spare Dear Heart the unpleasant task of cleaning out the mess, at least in part. And if she goes before I do, I won't have as much clutter with which I'll have to deal.

Keep a clean and neat kitchen. Nothing bespeaks neglect as eloquently as a sink full of dishes, cups, glasses, flatware, and pots and pans that need washing. You can make it a lot easier on yourself if you clean up as you go.

If you use a bowl and a whisk in preparing something for dinner, once you're done with the preparation wash them immediately and put them away. Same thing with anything used five or ten minutes before sitting down to eat what you've fixed for yourself. For example, if you use a knife to trim excess fat from the edges of a steak, wash and put away the knife before you put the steak under the broiler or on the grill. If you clean and straighten up as you go, you'll find the post-meal cleanup to be a snap.

Avoid kitchen clutter, too. Keep counter tops free of "stuff," because if you don't make an effort to do so you'll soon find you're out of room in which to go about the business of preparing meals. Keep handy at all times a roll of paper towels with which, among other things, you can wipe up or otherwise dispose of inevitable kitchen spills and disasters.

Finally, and again unless you can and want to hire help, accept the fact the only one who can assure you of livable digs is you. I promise you there's nothing unmanly about "women's work;" to the contrary, keeping your living quarters neat and tidy, keeping what you wear clean and neat, keeping both mental and physical rot at bay can be and is wonderfully rewarding. Not only does doing so make life a helluva lot easier, it keeps you in the game, verifies that you're still worth the price of admission.

10

FOOD FOR THE GANDER

At some point in his life, especially if he's on his own, or if his spouse either has become somehow incapacitated or simply has declared she's had it with meal-preparing, an old guy is faced with the likelihood he'll have to get himself something to eat. The choice is simple — either he eats restaurant food or prepares his own. The former quickly gets old, and the latter can be terrifying, usually because it has been tried with inedible or at best indifferent results.

What's more, if an old guy is a reader of newspapers and periodicals, or a watcher of television, he's bombarded by articles and program segments aimed at foodies, i.e., people who are food hobbyists, often food snobs who talk knowingly (or so it seems) of saffron and truffles, of Béarnaise sauce and vintage wines. Overhearing dedicated foodies playing a culinary version of "Can You Top This?" can cause the eyelids to ache.

You may scoff, but if you can read you can cook. Cook well, too, well enough to invite with confidence a guest or guests to dinner. Required are a few basic tools, time, patience, a little imagination, and some comprehensible guidance. Too often a cooking neophyte strolls into a bookstore and buys something by, oh, say, Julia Child, or some other food "authority." The beginner who does so is doomed to disappointment because an approach to Mrs. Child's menus, or the menus of any of the acknowledged food gurus, requires a certain grounding in the basics of food preparation.

Let's start with the necessary tools.

First and foremost, if you don't already have one, you need a sharp — let's repeat that, sharp — knife, preferably one called a cook's knife, especially a French cook's knife. Buy a quality knife, the steel of which is "soft" (e.g., old fashioned carbon steel) and thus amendable to repeated sharpening. Accompanying such a knife, buy a good stone or composite material sharpener, one that with a few swipes will give your knife blade an almost-razor like edge. While still at the cooking knife counter, buy a small paring knife, again one easily and readily sharpened.

Buy a counter top combination toaster/oven/broiler, a good one backed by a warranty of more than twenty minutes. Make certain it affords at least two rack positions and has a removable "dust" pan. Chances are you'll be cooking in small quantities and thus won't need a big oven. Besides, the smaller unit will save you money.

Shop around and find some good, solid-feeling but not necessarily heavy non-stick cookware — a frying pan, a sauce pan or two, a decent-sized pot, and a pot big enough to enable you to cook a pot roast or plunge into boiling water standard length spaghetti, linguine, perhaps even a chicken lobster.

Buy a small, round, and bake-proof stoneware crock and a couple of rectangular aluminum or heatproof glass pans in which you can roast or bake a variety of items, e.g., meatloaf. Get a ladle, a colander, a couple of big sauce spoons, a spatula or two, and two or three wooden spoons and at least one wooden spatula. Something you'll find handy is a combination wooden spoon and scraper called, oddly enough, a scraper spoon. Also, buy what's called a whisk; among other things, you'll use it to scramble eggs before cooking them. We'll assume you already have dishes, glasses, and flatware (knives, forks and spoons). All this washed, ready to go and within reasonable reach, we can take the first step.

What follows is based on the premise an old guy reading this has never so much as fried an egg.

Go to a grocery store or supermarket and buy a can of Campbell's condensed mushroom soup. I specify mushroom soup because you'll soon find it to be as essential to your budding cooking career as will be butter, dry white wine, and fresh lemon juice. Read the label and find out where to write for a copy of one or more of Campbell's cookbooks (e. g., Consumer Response Center, Campbell Soup Company, Campbell Place, Camden, N.J. 08103-1701, or if you use a computer inquire by e-mail — www.campbellsoup.com), especially a book devoted to recipes serving from two to four to six people. When you get the book, follow the directions to the letter. Don't try to ad-lib ingredients or amounts until you're reasonably sure of your ground. For example, if a recipe specifies a cup of cold water, don't — on the imagined theory you're making it more nutritious — substitute a cup of milk. Take it from one who learned the hard way, the people who put together the cookbook tried a cup of milk and found out it didn't work.

Following a divorce, and until I remarried, luckily to an excellent and enthusiastic cook, I embarked on my own kitchen career with a Campbell's cookbook entitled "Great Restaurants Cookbook, U.S.A.," which I'm reasonably sure is no longer in print. Thumbing through it the first time I found therein two or three recipes I thought I might manage to bring off. I wasn't a complete neophyte. I did know how to fry an egg, broil a hamburger, thaw and cook frozen peas, heat up a can of Dinty Moore stew, get myself a bowl of cereal . . . that sort of thing . . . but realized attempting anything beyond such no-brainers would place me in unfamiliar territory. Nonetheless, having tired of eating out, I was determined to take the culinary plunge. I mean, how hard could it be? At the time I was spending a weekend in a small rented cabin in New York State's Catskill mountains, and perhaps the proximity of nature combined with my solitude pushed me over the edge.

The first of the cookbook's recipes I tried was called Turkey Divan. I couldn't imagine myself buying and roasting a whole turkey, not even a turkey breast, and decided (fortunately as it turned out) chicken would do as well. Accordingly I bought a boned chicken breast, took the skin off and trimmed off the yellow fat, boiled a pot of water, added a pinch of salt and tossed it in. The recipe called for four individual dishes called casseroles, but all I had was a small, round stoneware crock. Following directions I coated the inside of the crock with butter, and when the chicken breast had cooked I sliced it up and lined the bottom of the crock with the slices. I then opened and spread atop the slices of chicken a package of once frozen but now thawed broccoli florets. Next I spooned over the broccoli and leveled off the entire contents of a 10.5 ounces can of Campbell's condensed cream of chicken soup. I topped all this with six or so generous slices of sharp cheddar cheese and popped the crock into the oven, which I had pre-heated to a specified 450 degrees. Again following the recipe's instructions, I left the crock in the oven for about 15 minutes, or until I could see the cheese had melted and was bubbling. I then took the crock out of the oven, placed it on a wire cooling rack and sprinkled its contents with a little freshly ground black pepper. Then I cleaned up the minor mess I had made in the cabin's tiny kitchen, careful, by the way, to wash with soapy water and wipe dry with paper towels all food preparation surfaces, especially the plastic cutting board upon which I had placed the raw chicken. (These days you can buy bleach-impregnated paper "cloths" that do an admirable job of keeping counter tops and cutting boards clean and bacteria-free, but here again pay particular attention to surfaces upon which you've placed raw chicken or fish).

While the chicken was cooking initially, I had set the table, complete with checkered red-and-white table cloth and a white linen napkin, even a glass for the jug white wine (Chablis) I had in the fridge.

So I'm ready, right? I transfer the crock and the rack it's sitting on to the table, grab a serving spoon with which to spoon out its contents, pour myself a glass of chilled wine and sit down. I hadn't given a thought to bread or rolls, or a salad, not even dessert; such refinements would come later in my budding culinary career. My total concentration was on what I had prepared, and I was delighted to discover my intensity was rewarded. It was, in a word, delicious, so much so I helped myself to seconds, musing as I ate that next I would try one of the shrimp recipes.

Thus began my brief career as a cook, my initial successes, thanks to that original cookbook, leading me to the preparation of sea bass *en papillote*, beef Wellington, apricot-glazed apple torte, peach cobbler, even such things as cold potato-leek soup as well as hollandaise sauce.

The high point in this entire experience came one night when still a bachelor I invited my fiancé, her daughter (later my stepdaughter), and a former boss and his wife to dinner. I served cold cooked artichokes with mustard-mayonnaise sauce, the sea bass en papillote, and a salad of fresh greens, all of it accompanied by a crisply cold French wine called *pouilly-fuisse*. Apple torte topped with a little fresh heavy cream was served as dessert, and I made a pot of espresso coffee and poured pony glasses of chilled French pear brandy called *poire William*. Finally pushing himself away from the table and looking around, a big and contented grin on his face, my former boss said, "This is my favorite French restaurant." Coming from that worthy, it was high praise.

This sort of undertaking may sound scary and far too elaborate, but it needn't be. The trick is to use fresh ingredients whenever possible, to take it step-by-step, and to abide by the KISS principle; i.e., "Keep It Simple, Stupid." If you do you'll soon learn what works and what doesn't, and you'll find yourself enjoying the preparation and eating of dishes you never imagined yourself cooking and consuming . . . things like mussels, crab cakes, corn fritters, warm potato salad, eggs benedict, oyster stew, steak tartare, and on and on.

Dedicated food preparation will, I promise you, enhance your life, will reward you in any number of ways, perhaps most importantly in terms of personal fulfillment. What's more, preparing your own meals also will give you the very desirable opportunity to monitor your diet, to make certain what you eat is properly prepared and is appropriately nutritious.

Most old guys extant these days were children of

the 1930s — that is, of the Depression — and a parental admonition that echoes in their ears is "Clean up your plate." If at any time they served in the military it's all but certain a wall in more than one chow hall featured a large-print admonition to "Take all you want, eat all you take."

Even given the tight, often extremely so, household budgets of the Depression, the "clean up your plate" mandate was dead wrong. Many a kid, me included, was forced to sit at table until he or she ate by-now-cold spinach or lima beans, in my case cauliflower and yellow squash. The rest of the family would have eaten their meal, been excused from the table and gone about their business, and there I'd be, alone, sobbing, dreading the choking down of stuff I loathed with all my heart. Sound familiar? It was enough to make one reluctant to come to the table at all, let alone sit down and eat. And too often it resulted in food hangups, holdovers from childhood that discouraged dining experimentation, the tasting of different cuisines, of so-called ethnic foods. One tended to settle into a food groove and never come out of it. When I hear an old guy say "I'm a meat-and-potatoes man," my heart goes out to him, for all along he has denied himself one of the genuine pleasures of being a human being. Thus it was years before I cottoned to cauliflower, a revelation resulting from a host serving it topped with melted cheddar cheese. Alternate slices of zucchini and yellow squash baked with a little butter in a small earthenware dish called a ramekin, topped with a sprinkling of nutmeg converted me on the spot. When former U.S. President George "Poppy" Bush made it known to the world that he loathed broccoli, it was the only time during his entire administration I felt sorry for him, sorry for what he had missed and was missing, steamed fresh broccoli drizzled with a little butter sauce being one of the delights of being alive.

Equally suspect is the urging to "Take all you want, eat all you take." The fact is that most portions served us, or that we serve ourselves, are too large. Pile on the mashed potatoes, shovel on the green beans, have some more, eat up, it's good for you. No it ain't. *All the food you need is enough to sustain good health*; the rest just adds weight and taxes the digestive system. Unless ordered by a doctor to do so for a specific purpose — e.g., addressing diabetes — avoid diets, especially diets holding out the rarely realized promise of losing weight. If what you have in mind is losing weight, eat less. Knock off so-called snacking. And keep things in balance. If at the dinner table you go overboard on a piece of creamy chocolate cake for dessert, for your next dessert, core, quarter and eat a Granny Smith apple, skin and all. If butter is an essential ingredient in a dish you prepare for yourself, "butter" your dinner bread or roll with a low-calorie cheese spread.

I'm a pushover for just about any kind of fruit pie and fight a battle within to cut myself no more than a modest piece. And I have to force myself to not have a second piece. But if in your progress as a cook you get around to baking a pie, spread the eating of it over several days; refrigerate it and it'll keep, and you won't be piling it on by feeling you have to eat it two or more meals running. Same thing with a cake.

By the way, don't laugh at the idea of baking your own pies, even your own cakes. Doing so is not for the overly cautious. The late Gene Fowler, a former newspaperman turned one of my favorite writers of books, reported that boyhood friend and later Hollywood neighbor Jack Dempsey often baked and sent over to the writer's house an apricot pie, the one-time heavyweight champion's favorite.

What's being repeated here as it applies to an old guy's intake of food is the old adage "Moderation in all things." If you eat a high-calorie meal one time, eat a low-calorie meal the next time. Balance things out. Cut down on the portions. Avoid overindulgence in the "killers" — butter, cream, cheeses, fatty meats (e.g., marbled steak), and so on. You can consume just about everything, including the "killers," but in small quantities. The rewards are not only good health, but also weight kept within bounds, enabling you to bend over to tie your shoes without feeling your eyes are about to pop out of your head.

11

SMOKE MOST FOUL

One of the absolute basics upon which the United States of America was founded concerns freedom of speech. The source of this tenet of American life was a sentiment perhaps best summed up in a quote attributed to the eighteenth century French writer Voltaire: "I disapprove of what you say, but I will defend to the death your right to say it." A summary exception to this most admirable principle was advanced by American jurist Oliver Wendell Holmes, Jr., who in a 1919 opinion wrote, "The most stringent protection of free speech would not protect a man in falsely shouting fire in a theater and causing panic."

A variation on the theme applies to the current brouhaha about smoking. Pertaining to free speech, Voltaire's assertion was and is unequivocal, but applying a variation of the same assertion to smoking muddies the waters.

Before going on I should tell you I was a smoker from age seventeen or so until I was fifty-three. I started out smoking a pipe but soon switched to gaspers, specifically Chesterfields, a brand loyalty fostered by the manufacturer's sponsorship of a fifteen-minute radio program featuring the music of the Glenn Miller Orchestra, of which at the time I was a devotee. For a brief period during World War II, when I was a bed patient in an Army hospital, my consumption of cigarettes was as much as three packs a day. But once I was up and around and had things to do other than read and smoke, I settled down to a pack, occasionally a pack-and-a-half, a day, a habit that held sway for the next thirty-five or so years. Over that same period of time I continued to smoke and inhale a pipe, and also admired and enjoyed (and inhaled) good cigars.

And then one day, while taking a stress test in the Norwalk, Connecticut, hospital, I passed out. Wired to various monitoring devices, I was huffing and puffing on a treadmill . . . and then I was on the floor surrounded by flashing lights, oscilloscope blips, and four anxious-looking attendants in hospital whites. Later, on my feet and feeling a bit wobbly but okay, I went to get dressed to go home. As I put on my shirt I took note of the pack of Kent filter cigarettes in the pocket thereof. Not hesitating a moment, not giving it a fraction of thought, I pitched that pack of butts into a nearby wastebasket and haven't smoked since.

Scared? You bet, although I admit I had been thinking about quitting for a year or more before I finally did. It was the little hacking cough that bothered me, that and the fact I didn't seem to have what I liked to think of as my usual stamina. And like the proverbial reformed drunk, I climbed aboard the anti-smoking bandwagon. Oh, I didn't buttonhole smokers in the street and urge them to accept the gospel of a smoke-free life, but if given the opportunity I wasn't above relating my own experience accompanied by assurances of how much better I felt, how much more I enjoyed my meals, slept better, how much more energy I had, that I no longer reeked of tobacco smoke, no longer had smokers breath, didn't burn holes in my ties and shirts, have a smelly ashtray on my desk, and on and on. No sir, I had reformed. I didn't smoke, but I certainly didn't mind if others chose to smoke.

My noble tolerance changed, however, when it became apparent that so-called secondhand smoke was almost as bad as the straight stuff. Over a very short span, tobacco smoke, especially from cigarettes, generated by others began to bother me. It could very well have been psychosomatic, but I felt my eyes watering, my breath somehow restricted. I craved fresh or at least uncontaminated air. Not the least bit "mental" was an awareness of secondhand smoke permeating my clothing; seated in a restaurant in which smoking was permitted, jackets and shirts (and my hair) quickly took on the reek of a smoker. My wife, a former smoker who one day had lunch with a group of her friends, some of whom smoked, afterward kept an appointment with a doctor, and when she replied in the negative to his asking her if she smoked, the doctor sniffed and allowed an expression of disbelief to cross his face.

I still tolerate smokers, but grudgingly. And not because, as spelled out above, their smoking annoys me, but because I'm concerned for their health, for their well being. As an old guy, as is so with any old guy, I learn by the day of friends and acquaintances checking out, a truly alarming number of them victims of lung cancer and/or heart disease. Frequently overheard at memorial services is, "Well, you know he was a heavy smoker."

I once went to a Veterans Administration hospital in Tampa and there saw pajama-clad ruins of men in wheelchairs coughing their guts out but still sucking away on cigarettes, one of them — ready? — through a tracheal tube.

Smoking is, admittedly, an addiction, a terribly strong addiction at that, and giving it up isn't easy. But if as an old guy you'd like to be around at least for the second half of a doubleheader, a positive step towards insuring such longevity would be to stop smoking. Sure, there are seemingly healthy ninety-plus-year-olds who have smoked all their lives, who continue to smoke, apparently impervious to the havoc within that smoking causes. But such men and women are exceptions, even freaks. For most of us the "filthy weed" is just that, a filthy weed, and we'd be wise to have no more to do with it.

As related, I quit "cold turkey." My wife tapered off with and quit thanks to nicotine chewing gum. Some people quit as a result of hypnosis (a result I question, tending to think the desire to stop smoking was in place long before some swami did his or her act), some as a result of wearing a nicotine patch. Some are able to quit by enrolling in a support group and following a twelve-step plan similar to that followed by recovering alcoholics. The means of quitting are as diverse as are smokers, but regardless of method the end is more than worth the effort required to get the cigarette (or cigar or pipe) monkey off your back.

Years ago, farm barns across this country often bore a painted legend urging those who saw it to "Chew Red Man." And not too long ago there was a vogue involving the use of "smokeless tobacco" called snuff. Both practices can be and often are lethal. Rotting gums, tooth loss, mouth cancers, to say nothing of foul breath, often are the result of using either chewing tobacco or using snuff. Any number of former major league baseball players are today wearing dentures or fighting gum disease because chewing tobacco was, and in some instances still is, the "macho" thing to do; it signified you had "made the show," i.e., become a big-leaguer. Quite apart from being a disgusting habit, the cancers caused by irritation to membranes of the mouth by chewing tobacco or using snuff, including tucking a small, porous envelope of mint-flavored snuff between cheek and gum, can metastasize into major league cancer. And cancer kills.

If chewing on something is a thing you simply have

to do, switch to sugarless chewing gum, even if you are an old guy for whom chewing gum is a bit whoopsie-do. Either that or buy yourself a cuddly teddy bear. Either way you'll save an impressive amount of money.

And put out that damned cigarette.

12

STAYING TUNED IN

Throughout the 1920s and early 1930s readers of certain of the nation's newspapers were treated to a series of cartoons and comic strips by an artist named Clare Briggs. One of his regular single-panel features was entitled "When a feller needs a friend." Usually depicted was some poor bloke in a situation in which a little help, understanding, or just plain compassion was called for. One of my favorites showed a callow youth standing in front of a bathroom washbasin giving himself his first shave as his parents and kid brother stood in the doorway looking on and smiling. Talk about self-consciousness!

I don't know what a friend, had one been handy, could have done for the young fellow other than close the bathroom door, but certainly the situation called for a bit of sympathy. After all, adolescent males groping toward manhood are among the more poignant participants in the passing parade.

At the other end of the life span are old guys who find themselves in awkward situations calling for help from a friend, but for whom no friend is at hand. An extreme example of such a situation has been depicted in TV spots showing an elderly woman who has fallen down and is unable to get up; all she can do is cry "Help" in the hope someone will hear her and come to her aid. Not so extreme but far more common, and more to the point, is the old guy who over time sheds himself of friendships and retreats into a sort of self-imposed exile. Examples are to be found everywhere — park benches, public libraries, "senior citizen" centers, cafeterias, what-have-you. You see them sitting by themselves, blank expressions on their faces, seemingly with no purpose in mind and with nothing to do but await their time to check out. Any one of them is a "feller" in need of a friend.

Unfortunately, too often old guys withdraw into this form of solitude by choice. In many instances they've lost their wives, become estranged from their children and simply have been unable to even partially fill the resultant void in their lives. Or they've become argumentative, obstinate, ornery, what earlier generations referred to as "crabby," and in deference to their views and opinions have washed their hands of old friendships, of any desire to make new friends. They fall into and eventually tend to wallow in a slough of bitterness. They become indifferent not only to others but to themselves — going unshaven, becoming careless about personal cleanliness and hygiene, just throwing something on to cover their nakedness and not giving a damn how they appear in the eyes of others.

These are old guys in need of a friend, even though any form of friendship offered may be rejected. Part of the problem is selfishness, of opting to drop out.

One of the more counterproductive aspects of modern life in this country is the phenomenon of "adults only" retirement communities, usually gated enclaves in which no one under the age of fifty-five is allowed to reside. If you want to withdraw from life, really want to get old in a hurry, you can't do much better than move into such a community. There you'll be surrounded by people of your own age and, broadly speaking, of like opinions. You'll be insulated, set apart from the hurly-burly of contemporary life. You'll fall into a pattern of easy routines, bolstered by the knowledge your peers are "folks just like us."

And your brain will turn to stone.

I loathe rock 'n' roll, rap, hip-hop, hate seeing young women defiled by tattoos, young men with tattoos, earrings, pierced eyebrows, a ring in the nose. I despair that so many young people hold themselves so cheaply. I despise all the "low rent" features of today's so-called popular culture, its lack of grace and wit. I can't believe how rude, how thoughtless of others so many of our young people seem to be. Yet I don't try to retreat from the ubiquitous cacophony and chaos of the junk that is their "music," and I do try to ignore their often anti-social behavior, their often bizarre appearances. I do so because, to again steal from comedian Flip Wilson's "Reverend LeRoy," it's "What's happenin' now." To run away from life as it is being lived is to run away from living. And the situation isn't nearly as bleak as anyone over the age of sixty-five tends to think it is.

I've found that talking baseball with a fifteen-year-old fan can be as rewarding as it is with a fellow geezer. A kid may never have heard of Pee Wee Reese, but his regard for Derek Jeter is no less enthusiastic. Too, you may discover, as I have, that when talking baseball, golf, wartime, history, old movies — just about anything providing it isn't done pedantically, as if you were lecturing — young people respond. They're curious, even eager to be told about bygone people and events. And in doing that sort of thing, of making an effort to put themselves in a position to do so if asked, old guys add both time and meaning to their lives, especially meaning. It isn't a matter of living vicariously through the lives of young people, but rather one of an old guy being in the swim, a decidedly different breed of fish, granted, but out there nonetheless, swept along with everyone else, old and young, in the tide of the day's events.

People who make gerontology their business assure us of the need to keep our minds active. They recommend that we do crossword puzzles, take up hobbies, do volunteer work, perform community service, and on and on. All well and good. But unless we feel good about what we're doing, that it's of importance as opposed to merely killing time, the effort is pointless and in fact may well push us into the pit of depression, imagined or clinical. If solving a crossword puzzle doesn't result in some form of inner zing, why bother? If any activity is simply going through the motions, the value of it is nil. What the gerontologists tend to slide over is that old guys — those who care, anyway — are as hungry for knowledge and insight as is any five-year-old. But the knowledge and the insight can't be dished out like so much Pablum; it has to have teeth, to have genuine worth. Teach a lifelong office clerk or a former Teamster to make a leather wallet, you've done him a disservice. On the other hand, lead him through the intricate work of making a saddle and you've taught him something he knows is of value, something that makes him feel you deem him as worthwhile, as something other than a patronized kid away at summer camp.

To befriend an old guy the approach should be straightforward, as an individual, and not as one of a segment of society. Ideally, an old guy should be someone who, with a certain steely look in his eye, cautions, "Watch out who you're calling a senior citizen, buster." I hate being addressed or dealt with as if I was anything other than what I am, gray-haired and getting on in years, perhaps, but no less involved in leading my life, no less baffled by the absurdities and indignities of the overall scene. I can cope with all that. What gets me is that so many old guys haven't a clue as to who or what they are. It's as if their old age had been dealt to them from the bottom of the deck.

In truth, a dullard who's a pain in the ass at age twenty-three tends to be a dullard and a pain in the ass at age sixty-three or seventy-three. These are the sort of people who plaster on the bumpers of their cars stickers reading "The Bible said it, I believe it, and that's that." Their convictions were formed early on, and nothing since has penetrated the rigidity of their minds. These also are people the rest of us should most fear — the ideologues, the absolute certainty advocates, the "My mind's made up; don't bother me with facts" set.

In the ranks of old guys, these types are legion. These are the people who vote clods, liars and crooks into office because they lack the imagination or the will to study those asking for their vote. Old guys, if they'd get off their mental backsides, have a great deal of political clout, have the voting booth power to genuinely affect change for the better, but they fail to exercise it because it's easier to vote for their party's choice, for the incumbent, the soothsayer, the stroker, the candidate who plays to their fears and prejudices. The rule of thumb, ideally, is the greatest good for the greatest number, but too often the perspective of old guys boils down to narrow self-interest.

Just one of the benefits of rubbing elbows with young people now and then, of really listening to what they have to say, is to appreciate that much of what they deal with in the course of their daily lives is familiar territory, has a familiar ring. For example, crying babies still need attending to, and dishes still have to be washed, car payments made, laundry done, groceries bought, meals prepared, and on and on . . . the same stuff with which old guys have coped all their adult lives. Yet this sort of thing isn't perceived as being on-going; rather, the old guy tends to divorce himself from the lives of those considerably younger than himself, feeling that he and only he has been through the crucible of getting from one day to the next. The cliché is the old guy who upon hearing of something says, "Let me tell you how it was when I was a boy. I had to get up at five o'clock in the morning to milk the cows, then I had to walk four miles . . . blah, blah, blah."

The peripherals change, the nitty-gritty doesn't, the point being that in a life sense, old guys have much if not everything in common with men fifty or more years younger. Surely I can't be the only old guy who to this day can hear his father telling him, "There's nothing you do or have done or will do that I haven't done, or thought of doing." What that sort of realization makes us is brothers, some young, some old, but essentially all in the same boat, and to deny that, to lay down our swords and shields and take refuge in drop-out isolation and bitterness, is to surrender all reason for being.

13

MEETING NEW PEOPLE

Inevitable in becoming an old guy is a change in the *dramatis personae* with whom the drama of one's life is played out. The important characters — family, for example — are likely to remain constant (granted, not always on speaking terms), but the peripheral players are all but certain to change. Men and women with whom an old guy worked for forty years fade from view and thus become yesterday's bananas. Good ol' knockaround buddy Harry relocates to Tucson and maybe is or is not heard from only through an annual Christmas card, or perhaps a birthday phone call. The neighborhood pub is knocked down and replaced by an Applebee's, and the guys with whom the old guy has gone fishing, played cards, or played golf for years and years have either died, succumbed to various ills and infirmities, or have moved away.

What this means is that an old guy is all but certain to meet never before known people, some of whom will be worth his time and attention, others wastes of both. The one overriding truth in this inevitability is that unlike a workplace, a club, a professional association . . . whatever . . . fools needn't be suffered, gladly or otherwise. An old guy has the luxury of selecting those with whom he plays or socializes. Besides, it's likely he hasn't the patience to put up with people for whom he feels no attraction and in whom he has no interest.

The fact is that most of the new people you, an old guy, are likely to meet will be of your own age, or at least of your generation. In many respects this is good, mainly in that such people are likely to know what you're talking about. Thus you don't have to explain who Jack Benny was, or that War Admiral was a race horse and not commander of the Pacific fleet during what TV's Archie Bunker referred to as " . . . WWII, the Big One . . . it was all in the papers." But the flip side of this coin toss is that many of these new people of your own generation are windy bores, or are dishwater-dull. Even worse, some of them are bullshitters, people — men usually — who've been bullshitters so long they've lost sight of the truth (as opposed to out-and-out liars, who at least are aware they're lying and perhaps anticipate some form of retribution; bullshitters, on the other hand, are bulletproof).

Mentioned earlier was the guy with a bumper sticker reading, "The Bible said it, I believe it, and that's that." Of the same breed is the fellow who forty years ago became either a Republican, a Democrat, or whatever, and ever since hasn't bothered to inquire as to what his party of choice is up to. Accordingly, an administration dominated by one party or the other can be a disaster, yet the guy remains oblivious to its shortcomings, its insensitivities, its downright gaffes and failures. Such people are and remain alarmingly uninformed, are mentally lazy and thus unworthy of your attention. They're the kind of people who by speaking three consecutive sentences can make your eyelids droop, or who start a comment by saying, "I see where that [insert racial slur] . . ." *Click!* Off goes your listening switch and it's on to wondering what you're going to have for dinner.

You haven't time for such people, haven't time to listen to their inanities, their prejudices, the outpouring of their concrete minds. It isn't a matter of being impolite, but rather of not wanting to be overwhelmed and suffocated by the dust and debris of other people's mental claptrap.

Where do you find interesting people, people with whom you might enjoy talking and spending time, people preferably but not necessarily age peers? It can depend upon what you like to do. I've been a golfer all my life, more often than not on public golf courses, meaning I've often been paired with strangers, with people I've never seen before and am not likely to ever see again. Most of them have been just that, people I haven't seen since. But some of them now are among my small circle of friends, people in whom I've been rewarded to discover common interests, a like sense of humor (especially a like sense of humor).

I don't recall the context but do recall playing in a foursome of strangers, and over a putt on about the fourth hole having cause to mention long ago heavyweight boxing champion Bob Fitzsimmons. "Ah, yes," said one of the group, "Ruby Robert, he of the infamous 'solar plexus' punch." It turned out that this guy, like me, knew the names of every heavyweight champion dating back more than a hundred years to the reign of John L. "The Boston Strong Boy" Sullivan. We formed an instant bond and nattered away on a variety of subjects throughout the rest of the round, his mind being as cluttered with trivia as was and is mine. Unfortunately, he was a winter visitor to Florida from Milwaukee and I never saw him again and have no idea what happened to him. But had he been within reach I know we'd have become friends.

If you're a reader you're likely to find your counterparts in the nearest library. Books open worlds of possibilities, and people who read them are apt to be considerably more interesting than the people happy to tell you that never in their lives have they read a book. Further, many libraries offer seminars and discussion groups on a variety of subjects, and if such a session is on a subject in which you're interested, you're certain to meet people with a similar interest.

My father was a lifelong and not overly successful student of the running horse, and over the years of his patronage of Metropolitan New York race tracks became friends with a number of fellow punters and employees of the New York Racing Association (NYRA) and its concessionaires, people he saw and spoke with only on the days he went to one of the tracks. Yet he knew what they had done with most of their lives, where they lived, whether or not they were married and had children, and so on, all or much of the minutia of friendships. Following a day at a track he would relate something one of his friends told him, some detail that to us, usually just my mother and me, made the person of whom he was speaking seem like someone we knew almost as well as he did. Thus when at the track, and apart from the races themselves, he was never lonely, never bored; there was always someone — an usher, a bartender, a fellow punter — with whom he could and would chat.

The point being made here is that to meet people with whom you'd like to spend time you have to go out among them, keeping in mind that the truism that no one is going to beat a path to your door is especially true of lonely old guys.

The trap in all this is that you're likely to meet a lot of rejects before you strike pay dirt. Don't be surprised if after even months of friendship something happens, or something is said that tells you you've been riding the wrong horse. Foul jokes don't do much for me, and after a guy tells me the third or fourth dirty story I cross the street when I see him heading in my direction. Racial slurs aren't in my bag either; when I hear one, my consciousness switch goes to the "Off" position and I start looking for an exit. I don't have to put up with this form of stupidity and neither do you. It's not rude to turn your back on a bigot, and you don't have to say anything; you can just walk away, determined to avoid any future contact with such a person.

There's a subtle twist in all this, however. Some of those you meet will say or do things aimed at shocking you, perhaps even testing you. You have to decide on the spot whether what you know about that person at the moment makes it worthwhile to continue the relationship. A man I know, a retired career military type, habitually employs ethnic and racial slurs, but it's part of his old curmudgeon act, for if anyone, regardless of "race, creed, color, or country of national origin" was injured or in need of ten dollars to tide him or her over, this guy would be the first to dig in his pocket or come to that person's aid. There are more of these types among us old guys than you might think likely, so be prudent and patient in your judgments, weighing carefully the worth to you of the total person.

Avoid whiners, people for whom the sun never shines, flowers never bloom, humor is unknown. When I was young and someone I knew met me in the street and asked how I was, I always wanted to get right in his face and open my mouth as if at the dentist and complain of an impacted wisdom tooth, or some similar dental disaster. My thought then and now was that the person asking me how I was really wasn't interested in my state of mind or health, but merely was making conversation. I've done it and do it myself. Now, however, I find that some people my age, when I run into them and ask how they are, will rattle off a recital of woe about everything from physical ills to high taxes and thoughtless children. Such people have a lot of baggage to unload, but I refuse to be an available porter, and so should you.

Often cited is the bromide, "Be careful of what you wish for because you just might get it." A take on that might work out as, "Be careful of those from whom you seek friendship, because it's possible they could become your enemies." I once worked as a press agent for showman Mike Todd, and on more than one occasion he would say, "God save me from my friends. I know all about my enemies."

14

COPING WITH STRESS

Apart from heart attacks and cancer in its various forms, the great killer in modern life may well be stress. In fact stress may be a more than significant factor in the former, and it certainly does nothing to ease the agonies and the heartbreak of the latter. The truly unfortunate thing about stress, however, is that often it's self-imposed; we have a tendency to create monsters where none exist.

For younger men, stress stems from many things — job pressures, money worries, errant offspring, dipping one's wick where it shouldn't be dipped, caring or providing for elderly parents, health concerns . . . the list seems almost endless. It manifests itself in any number of guises — sleepless nights spent tossing and turning, failure to achieve or maintain tumescence, stomach distress, a flagging appetite, quick to anger, withdrawal from family and friends . . . again, the list seems almost endless.

For old guys, stress takes on closer-to-the-bone forms — money, food, waning physical capacities, loneliness, medicinal needs, renal and bowel woes, getting to appointments on time, the loss of one's driver's license, car trouble, the deaths of friends and loved ones.

A younger man can view stress with some hope of surmounting it — a bullying and incompetent boss may be replaced (i.e., fired or, more likely, promoted), the mythical ship may at last come in, the teenage son may stop smoking dope, the car's air conditioner may just need a new hose and not "a whole new unit," the pregnant girlfriend may have a miscarriage, the mother in a nursing home seemed rational the last time she was visited, the new putter may cure his yips, maybe the growth on his arm isn't cancer after all, and so on.

An old guy, on the other hand, tends to be short on hope. He knows that unless he hits the lottery there's not much chance of his ever having more money at his disposal, knows no one other than himself cares that he may be sweating the source or content of his next meal, that the cancer isn't going to "go away," that bladder control can be a now-and-then thing, that the barrel of abandoned putters in the garage represent lost hopes, that the likelihood of replacing lost friends is nil, that the cost of his prescription drugs won't go down, that failing eyesight isn't likely to improve, that the car's air conditioning system is certain to require "a whole new unit," that morning stiffness is everywhere but where he'd like it to be, and so on.

All this being so, the question becomes how does an old guy deal with stress? Obviously there are no easy answers, but there are certain steps that can be taken, certain adjustments that can be made.

Let's start with money, with income. If you find

yourself living up to and on occasion even beyond what you have coming in each month, it's time to sit down with paper and pencil and determine exactly where your money is going. It may be that relocating to more affordable housing is called for, or that the luxury car, even an old one, and its thirst for premium gasoline should be replaced by a runs-on-regular compact. Having convinced yourself you'd be an absolute dub in a kitchen, perhaps you're spending too much on restaurant food as opposed to preparing your own meals. It could be that you're an impulse buyer, someone who buys at first sight without giving thought to the ultimate use or worth to you of what you're buying.

For example, when digital cameras first came out, a guy I know paid big bucks for one, his thought being he'd take photos, would crank them into his computer and send them via the Internet to his kids, who lived in Oregon. And he did just that . . . for about three weeks before realizing he had nothing more to photograph that might remotely interest the kids. The upshot is that another impulse buy sits unused in a drawer.

Many years ago I had a friend named Charlie Scholes, who at the time was director of aviation for the Humble Oil Company. One day we were flying in what I recall was a twin Beech of some sort, and I said I thought it was a good airplane.

"Yeah," said Charlie in his Texas drawl, "as long as

it's movin'. Otherwise, it's just eatin' money."

That's how it is with a lot of what we manage to accumulate over the years, stuff that is rarely used but sits on shelves or in drawers "eatin' money," or at least taking up space. I have a pile of old phonograph records, 78s I haven't played in more than thirty years. In truth, I don't even have a record player. The records, however, take up shelf space I could use for my overflow of books. *Overflow!* Hah! I have books upon books that haven't been cracked in forty years, and I can't tell you why I hold onto them. When I die, I know my wife or my sons are going to shovel most of them out the door, so why do I hold onto them? I don't know, but I do know I should prune them and simplify my life.

And there's the key to fending off stress — *simplifying your life.* It doesn't mean dropping out, withdrawing from the hurly-burly of getting from one day to the next. Rather, simplifying your life means eliminating as many as possible of the things that tend to complicate the life of a typical old guy, things such as time payments; obligations for which, in truth, you no longer feel obligated; remembering really meaningless birthdays and anniversaries; maintaining semblances of friendship with people in whom, deep down, you've lost interest. That sort of thing, the lot of it so much emotional baggage you'd be far better off throwing out with the trash.

A source of very real stress for a single old guy can

be the stirrings of romance. John Widower meets Jane Widow, and John starts fantasizing a life of golden serenity that just possibly might be lived with Jane. He allows his imagination to get the better of him, lets it cloud his judgment. He ignores his instincts. After all, he feels he's in pretty good shape for a guy his age, and her demeanor reminds him of Don Marquis' Mehitabel the Cat in that "there's a dance or two in the old girl yet."

First thing John knows he's being asked to pick up Jane's daughter's dry cleaning. He goes along with that kind of thing for a bit, and then the water starts getting deeper and he's in "the romance" up to his neck, seemingly committed to an extent he hadn't anticipated. Suddenly he's not sleeping as well as he did, and his daughter and her husband start emitting periodic and politely disguised bleeps meant to indicate "Danger." And then Jane suggests wardrobe changes, that he should have his house painted, that he really needs a new sofa, that the wallpaper in his foyer needs replacing. In other words, poor ol' John starts jumping through hoops, in the process experiencing the sort of stress he had reason to believe was behind him.

We all need something going against the grain, something to keep us awake, something that, yes, irritates us, even if only mildly. It can be government of any stripe, certain people, certain aspects of popular culture, a certain newspaper columnist, a television program . . . anything that every now and then irks us, that sets our teeth on edge.

But none of these things are what I mean by stress. They may in fact increase our output of bile, bile we may well vent in the direction of any available ear, but they won't cause our palms to sweat, won't create within us feelings of obligation or of dread. About all the stress an old guy should have to face is getting suited up for the game of getting from one day to the next. Anything other than that is apt to find him reaching for the Rolaids.

No, whistling while walking past a figurative cemetery in the dead of night won't ease your anxiety, but it doesn't take much imagination to find another route to where you want to go. If something in your life is threatening, even vaguely so, and you sense it, are aware of it, make other arrangements. You're under no obligation to go somewhere you really don't care to go, you don't have to put up with people with whom you're uncomfortable, and you don't have to tolerate situations with which you're not in harmony. You don't want to be rude, of course, and you can express your appreciation of being asked, but if going to the Kiwanis Club fish fry is something you'd rather not do, it's absolutely okay to say, "No, thanks. I think I'll just stay put and read my book." The only exception here may be a plea from a grandchild of whom you're fond, and while at the fish fry you have to work at keeping in mind he or she is why you're there, for once you allow yourself to ask, "Why did I agree to come to this thing?" you're lost, and the experience is diminished for both you and, more importantly, for the child.

Even as an old guy you're going to encounter stressful situations. It's called being alive. But you can handle them if you keep in mind that remaining mountains to climb are few in number, that the life stakes at age seventy aren't nearly as high as they were at age forty, that you've pretty much weeded out the windbags, the bores and the bullshitters, that your friends on Tuesday are going to be your friends on Wednesday, and that any worthwhile female in your life isn't likely to count on you to do your Saint George act and slay her dragons.

15

THE PET TRAP

It's not uncommon these days to pick up a newspaper or a magazine, especially a magazine dedicated to "family living," that doesn't include in its contents at least one piece on the salubrious effect of pets on seniors, especially those living out the string in some form of communal living arrangement. TV likes the premise as well; we've all seen at least a half-dozen local programming features in which Bowser is seen in a nursing home licking the smiling face of some poor old geezer, the voice-over assuring viewers that Mr. Doe and Bowser have become fast friends, and that both look forward to the dog's weekly visits.

The upside in all this, of course, apart from the few minutes of companionship Bowser affords, is that Mr. Doe isn't called upon to water, feed, bathe, or clean up after the dog. It's what is known, petwise, as a win-win situation — the people-friendly dog gets to do its stuff, and the beneficiary of its outgoing personality is spared the job of caring for it.

It's quite true dogs, and in some instances cats (although the expression "cool cat" is not without significance), can manifest sincere affection for and devotion to human beings. Any number of old people in the world are thus attached, the pets presumably filling perceived voids in their lives. Two of my immediate neighbors are retired widowers, both of whom have a dog from which, presumably, they derive both pleasure and companionship. I also see them out walking the dogs, on occasion in the rain, or, living as we do in South Florida, in heat that would fell a moose.

Owning a pet is a two-way street — in exchange for a wagging tail and an exuberant greeting, or a contented purr while curled up in a lap, the proprietor must provide food and water, cleanliness, exercise, veterinary care, and, yes, companionship. A pet left to its own devices for hours on end soon gets the message — it's not as important to the owner as the owner is to it — the result often being off-the-wall behavior. Legion are pet-owners who've returned home after a day or night afield to find furniture damaged, clothes scattered about, a water dish upset, a pantry in disarray, a foul-smelling mess on the living room carpeting . . . whatever.

An old guy on his own and thinking of getting himself a dog or a cat should appreciate he's taking on a responsibility, specifically responsibility for the animal's life. Apart from the obvious, what that means is the surrendering of a certain degree of freedom. You'll have to get home "to feed the dog," for example, or if you're at last determined to take that long-promised cruise to Alaska, there's the dog to be cared for while you're gone. Placing a dog in a public kennel not only can be expensive, the care it receives can be either proper or indifferent, in some instances downright neglectful, perhaps even harmful. Kenneling your pet opens the door to certain traumas — your anxiety regarding the care it is receiving in your absence, the pet's in its sudden removal from familiar surroundings and equally sudden loss of contact with the human being upon whom it has learned to rely.

For a number of years I had a cat named Mrs. Nice. She was one of a litter born to a stray in a Catskill mountain cow barn. Soon aware that, as a country cat with a lot of competition, she was on the rough hustle, she staked out my then-wife and me, exercising all her feline wiles and charms to make sure we got the message: she wanted to be adopted. At first never brought inside our cabin, she quickly learned that making herself visible when one of us was about usually resulted in her being poured a saucer of milk, maybe even a little chopped up beef kidney (the latter soon became her diet of choice). Almost before we were aware of it, the cat, now spayed and given all her prescribed shots, was traveling back and forth between the cabin and our midtown Manhattan apartment. She hated the travel, but what were we to do, leave her on her own around the cabin from Sunday night to Friday night?

What I'm getting to is that without being fully aware of the consequences of doing so, we took on what turned out to be an obligation. Just as car seats and strollers are loaded into the car whenever a young family drives even crosstown to grandma's house, I found myself making sure the cat's kitty litter pan and her blanket were in the car whenever we drove back and forth.

The impact of this folly was brought home in spades when the lady and I divorced and went our separate ways; I now had custody of Mrs. Nice. I didn't have the heart to turn her out, have her put down, yet on more than one occasion I found myself required to cut short something I was enjoying doing in order to attend to the cat. Perhaps she may have been even more independent than she seemed to be and perhaps wouldn't have minded being on her own for another few hours or so, but I never felt free to take that chance. It was Mrs. Nice's dinner time, give or take an hour or so either way, and I felt obligated to deliver as my proprietorship of her implied.

On one occasion, upon returning from a country weekend, I drove my car up the ramp of the parking garage in which I kept it, and when I opened the driver's side door to get out so the attendant could take over, Mrs. Nice bolted for freedom. The parking garage was several blocks from my apartment house, so the cat was loose in a semi-rough neighborhood with which I was only marginally familiar. I can still see and hear myself walking up and down comparatively strange streets crying "Here, kitty kitty!" More than once over the next two or three days and nights I searched for the cat, and before some neighborhood kids I enlisted in the search found her and brought her home, I found myself thinking, "What in hell are you doing out here looking for a damn cat, especially one that took off on you?"

Years ago humorist James Thurber wrote that a dog lover was a dog in love with another dog. But humans tend not to think of it that way; instead, we learn to love our pets, and like all love it can lead to nutty behavior.

Look, it can be anything — dog, cat, parrot, budgie, goldfish . . . whatever, it has to be cared for and attended to, and if you own it you're elected to do the caring, to pay the required attention.

All along here one of the tenets for an old guy has been the simplification of life, the avoidance of stress. As much as a pet may brighten an old guy's days, it also complicates his life, perhaps not overly so but certainly undeniably so. So if you're thinking of acquiring a pet, think through — really think through — all the implications.

And there's this: Suppose one of my widower neighbors meets a really nice woman for whom he feels the first twinges of possible romance, someone with whom he thinks he'd genuinely like to hold hands for the rest of his life, but it turns out she's allergic to or simply can't abide dogs. What does he do? Where does he turn? What happens to the dog? Resentment City, right? If not fairly early in the relationship, likely down the road there'll come a time when, in a fit of pique, he'll say, "Damn it, you made me get rid of old Bowser!"

Here again is the wisdom of being thoughtful and careful of what you wish for.

16

THE KIDS AND YOU

Something around which pundits have danced since the beginning is the relationship between parents and children. Parents, having brought children into the world, are charged with loving them and with the care and feeding of them until the kids are of an age to strike out on their own. Ah, would that it were that simple.

Andy Rooney, television's resident curmudgeon, in a long ago "60 Minutes" piece on the plight of public schools in this country pointed out that the trouble wasn't so much crumbling buildings and lousy teachers as it was lousy parents. Specifics weren't forthcoming, but any regular reader of a daily newspaper knows the drill — uncaring parents, absentee parents, stupid parents, abusive parents, runaway parents, drunks, junkies, deadbeats, trollops, screw-ups . . . the usual detritus afflicting the human panoply. The odd thing about these sorts of people, however, is that although they're failures as parents and as people, and thus tend to issue forth clones of themselves, every now and then they produce an exemplary child, a kid who somehow manages to surmount the odds against him or her. A kid who escapes a sordid and deprived childhood has every good and just reason to sever ties to the mutt or mutts who brought him or her into the world.

The other side of the coin is that good, caring parents can produce duds, even monsters, the latter so-called bad seeds, kids who somehow manage to thwart or refute every attempt to guide them into lives as useful, aware, loving, and contributing members of society. In this kind of filial relationship there are more than enough scars to go around.

The concern here, however, is with old guys, some of whom have done a poor job of parenting and as a result are as neglected as they themselves were neglectful, some who have tried too hard and continue to do so with the result they're intrusive, and some who through luck and instinct managed to raise kids with whom they're still on a cordial, perhaps even mutually respectful and admiring footing. Unfortunately, the latter category of old guys is in short supply.

What's called for here is a lot of self-honesty. If you've been physically or mentally "on the road" for most of your kids' lives, you can't expect to be welcomed to their hearths as if you were a constant in their childhood and adolescence. Kids are remarkably hep to how they stand in the estimations of those they're around, and if over the years of their growing up you've been too busy to give them the attention and the affection they crave, as adults they'll more than likely treat you as they've been treated; i.e., indifferently. You can tell yourself you "did it all for them so they'd have nice clothes and a nice house to live in and food on the table and blah, blah, blah," but any kid worth his or her salt would happily wear gunnysacks and live in a tent with a parent or parents they know in their bones loves them, genuinely loves them and takes care of them.

So as an old guy, before you start moaning about never seeing or hearing from your kid or kids, you have to weigh thoughtfully your relationship to them as they were growing up. Keep in mind that indifference breeds indifference, and if indifference was your M.O. as a parent, you can't expect much more than that from your progeny.

One of the great schisms between parents and children is the clash of wills, not just the day-to-day stuff, but the parental determination that Johnny is going to be a bio-chemist whereas Johnny likes to tinker with cars and hopes to one day own a garage. For example, I know of a man who owned and ran a successful insurance agency he was determined would one day be owned and run by his son. But the kid liked to work with wood and hoped one day to become a carpenter or a cabinetmaker, trades the father deemed beneath his son. So the father forced the kid into the insurance business, and by age forty the kid was an unhappy divorced dipso hanging on by a thread before dropping to the oblivion of Skid Row. No one knows for sure, of course, but chances are that instead of becoming a drunk the kid might well have been a successful, or at least a happy carpenter. Anyhow, the father now is a bitter old man grappling with the certain knowledge he should have let his son be his own man rather than trying to make the kid into a carbon copy of himself.

Perhaps hardest of all for an old guy to accept is that a son or daughter just plain doesn't like him, or that a son-in-law or daughter-in-law doesn't like him and that his kid has opted to go along with his or her spouse. The cause can be petty — "I hate those stinky cigars he insists on smoking," "His table manners make me ill," "He never goes anywhere without that smelly old dog." Or the cause can be world-class — "The stingy bastard never gave me so much as a dime." "He treated my mother like dirt." "He's always mooching something," "I don't like the way that lecherous old goat looks at our Jennifer." The *causus belli* here can become even more horrendous.

Hard-nosed truth is that when one has reached old guy status it's hard to mend fences, especially with kids who give every indication of preferring that you keep your distance. And it's hard to bridge a marked intellectual gap, or a gap that exists between, say, a sharecropper dirt farmer and his big city brain surgeon son, his marketing executive daughter. Very often parent and child move and live in different worlds, and to pretend both are in one big happy familial mix is to all but guarantee disappointments and broken hearts. No one is to blame here; it's just the way things sometimes work out. The sharecropper should be proud of his brain surgeon son, and the brain surgeon should recognize that his sharecropper father was dealt a different hand yet is no less deserving of respect and affection because he never amounted to much. It doesn't mean they have to make like theirs is a formatted father-son relationship. It isn't and it never will be, so the old guy in the picture shouldn't wallow in an imagined slough of neglect.

Perhaps even more devastating than not being liked by your kids is not liking them. No one knows how many estranged families there may be in this country, but certainly the rock 'n' roll culture, for one thing, and the prevalence of illegal drugs, for another, and what seem to be handmaidens of both — lemming-like antisocial behavior and attitudes, blatant hype, cruel exploitation, the suspension of common sense, studied self-mutilation and disfigurement in one form or another (tattoos, nose rings, deliberate scarring . . . whatever), promiscuity, the dearth of wit and grace, single-minded greed, blatant materialism, and so on — have rendered more families asunder than ever did mere mortality. It's hard to work up much regard for an offspring who defiantly strays far from the fold and its lifestyle tenets. Kids lost to the streets or to a scruffy "let it all hang out" lifestyle may someday resurface, but when they do there's little if any hope something like a normal parent-child relationship can be restored.

As an old guy you can't dwell on this sort of breach.

What's done has been done, and nothing you do or say can put a secure lid on your hurt, your anger, your disappointment. Even if you resume some sort of "normal" relations with a once estranged child you'll never really be able to invest in that relationship your complete, unfettered trust; always in your mind, just under the surface, will be what to you is his or her betrayal. So don't brood about it. The choices, however inappropriate, have been made and can't be reversed, not entirely, anyway. And remember, once a kid who throughout his or her adolescence has told you to stuff it reaches the age of twenty-one, perhaps even sooner, you are under no obligation to give that child shelter, provide sustenance, or pick up tabs.

Finally, there's distance. You live wherever, and the kid or kids live thousands of miles in the other direction. Careers, jobs, marriage choices, wanderlust, anything can put virtually insurmountable distances between you and your children, and, perhaps of even more significance, their children as well. In my own instance, one son and his family live in Italy, another son and his family in England. A stepson and his family live in northern California. What this has meant to my wife and me is that all these years we're been dressed in our grandma and grandpa suits with no place to go. I have a granddaughter in college in England that to date I've seen exactly three times; she's a stranger to me. Same thing with a namesake adult grandson; I've seen him three times since he was born. When my wife and I built our house in Florida we also specified a swimming pool, telling ourselves that not only would we enjoy it, but wouldn't it be great to have a pool when our kids and their kids visited us. So far the pool has been used all of twice by the European grandchildren, and once by the California grandchildren.

There's no estrangement in any of these relationships. We communicate back and forth — telephone calls, e-mail, letters — and to the best of my knowledge we like each other. However, we lead different lives, have different interests, different associations, the result being that even though on cordial, even loving terms, we're essentially strangers.

It would be easy to shed tears over this *de facto* reversal of my imagined role as a grandfather — trips to Disney World, going to ballgames, teaching a grandson to fly-fish, going camping, shopping for school clothes, learning to hit a 7-iron, helping with homework, answering innumerable questions, reading to them, and so on — but to what end? My grandpa suit notwithstanding, nothing is going to bring my far-flung grandchildren any closer to me, and any future meetings we might have will of necessity have to start pretty much from scratch. So it's not what I had in mind. So what? I'm not the first grandfather to feel more or less irrelevant, and there's no point in stewing about it. As the Brits say, press on regardless.

17

KEEP ON TRUCKIN'

For many years members of the National Rifle Association have enjoyed — yes, enjoyed — telling anyone who'd listen that their firearms would be surrendered only when they were pried from their cold, dead hands.

Similar sentiments are expressed by old guys reluctant to give up their license to drive a car. It's almost as if being deprived of the driving privilege is an ominous prelude to going to that Great Automobile Junkyard in the Sky — "If I can't drive a car, I may as well be dead."

The fact is if any number of them *don't* give up their licenses they're going to die in car accidents, in the process often taking the lives of innocent others with them. Rarely does a day go without a story in the papers about some old gee whose faulty depth perception had him pulling out into traffic and being killed or severely injured as a result of being plowed into by an oncoming vehicle. Although many old guys don't like to drive yet feel they must, there comes a time in one's life when being behind the wheel is both a personal and public menace.

Cars, motor vehicles of any sort, are a convenience, yes, and they afford us desirable mobility. But what they really are, deep down, are manifestations of freedom, fast and powerful extensions of the freedom perhaps first experienced on a scooter, on the seat of a childhood bicycle, or on the back of a horse. So what an old guy forced to surrender his driving license is sacrificing, then, is a lot more than convenience and mobility; what he feels he's being deprived of is his freedom. More than any other consideration, it is the awareness of freedom that keeps so many gaffers on the roads long after they've lost the ability to drive well and safely.

How do you know it's time to "hang 'em up?" Fortunately, fate — or something — provides premonitions:

You're driving toward a crossroads at which you want to turn left, so a half-mile or more beforehand you pull over into the left lane and there you stay put, often at considerably less than the posted speed limit. Doing so fairly screams at you: "You're too timid to drive, your reflexes are too slow, and you've lost confidence in your ability to cope with traffic."

You're driving along thinking back to the night a girl named Clarissa first allowed you to unbutton her blouse and you drive through a STOP sign, or a red light. You may or may not hit or be hit, but you're dramatically made aware that in such an instance concentration on what you're doing has been suspended. You promise yourself it won't happen again, but don't bet it won't.

One of the troubles old guys have with what we think of as routine tasks is just that — they're routine;

we've performed them so many times in our lives we've ceased thinking about them. This explains why things such as toothbrushes, combs, razors, tools, cakes of soap, paper clips, pencils, ballpoint pens, sheets of paper, knives and forks, what-have-you seem to have a will of their own and fly out of our aging hands. We're so used to handling them we fail to go through a pick-'em-up-and-hold-onto-'em thought process. Once we've decided to, say, comb our hair, we don't bother to think what's required; by-now-instinctively we reach for the comb and are surprised when thanks to mishandling it it flies out of our hand. In reaching for it we've barely bothered to so much as glance at it.

There are other indications in which routine does us in. For example, I make myself a cup of tea each morning; i.e., I heat a cup of water in the microwave, then dunk in it a tea bag and stand by until the tea brews. Beforehand I will have downed a small glass of orange juice and perhaps made myself a bowl of cereal. I've done this drill so many times I'm pretty sure I could run through it blindfolded. Imagine the shock, then, to say nothing of the ludicrousness of one morning pouring orange juice into my tea cup and popping it into the microwave. As mentioned earlier, we laughingly refer to this sort of thing as absentmindedness, or as "having a senior moment," but the reality is "'Tain't funny, McGee."

What about so-called senior moments occurring

when an old guy is behind the wheel of his car, motoring along smartly at a brisk forty miles-per-hour? What if he has a "senior moment" and drives through a red light, or without thinking or looking pulls into a different lane and causes some other motorist to jump the curb and run into a light pole?

Old guys have to face the reality of diminished capacities. You may have been a virtual Mario Andretti as a young man, but now, unless you can claim honestly to be as good a driver as you ever were, you're a semi-guided missile, a menace both to yourself and to others.

So what's the alternative? There are a few, none of them on a par with the freedom of automotive mobility advancing age has forced you to surrender, but nonetheless useful. They boil down to family, friends, various forms of public transportation, or walking, what used to be referred to as "shank's mare."

You have to determine your basic transportation needs — a food market, a pharmacy, a doctor, a dentist, a dry cleaner, maybe a laundromat . . . whatever. If family or friends aren't available to take you to and fro on a desirable schedule, or if you'd turn blue rather than have anyone think you were imposing on them, the alternative is walking or public transport, which is to say a bus, courtesy van, subway (metro), or taxi. If cabs are a bit rich for you, if courtesy van comings and goings are hit-and-miss, or if you have to walk more than a half-mile or so to get to a subway or bus stop, then it's time to think about relocating to digs more accessible to means of scheduled public transportation. The thought of packing up and moving "in town" may terrify you, but being able to get about beats the hell out of involuntary (and often solitary!) confinement.

While we were deciding where we wanted to build our Florida house, my wife and I lived on the second floor of an apartment complex. Living alone in the apartment under ours was an elderly woman we gathered from what little she revealed to us had been a good time gal whose protector, years ago, had traded her in for a newer model. This poor abandoned soul had no one, no family other than a semi-retarded daughter married to an itinerant and uncaring con man, her only companion a bottle of Seagram's Seven from which she nipped throughout the day. Even sober she couldn't walk very well, and to get both the booze and what little food and essentials she required she depended for transportation on the complex's handyman, who while a genial and accommodating soul nonetheless charged her x-number of dollars per outing. Accordingly, and because she was on a very tight budget, her forays afield were undertaken only when absolutely necessary. She couldn't afford a movie, for example, and even had she had a little discretionary income there was no way to for her to get out to spend it. Things such as free concerts, free art exhibitions, free lectures, access to a public library, even an occasional trip to a shopping mall to sit and people-watch were denied her. Eventually, thanks to the booze, her liver started to bang and soon thereafter she died, almost literally a prisoner of her inability to get out and around, to remain interested in being alive.

As old magazine ads used to caution, "Don't let this happen to you." If the time comes when it no longer is safe for you to operate a car, or when the law forces you to become a pedestrian, make whatever arrangements are necessary to ensure your continued mobility. If you are confined to a wheelchair, or are otherwise limited in your ability to get out and about, call local social service agencies and inquire about the availability of transportation services for the handicapped. And don't turn up your nose at the thought of being lumped in a bus or a van with people in wheelchairs, people with seeing-eye dogs, people who are mentally handicapped. Keep focused on the main goal, which is to continue your role as someone among those present, as someone free to move about in a normal course of getting from one day to the next.

The alternative is or can be ever-diminishing capacities and a lonely, bitter end.

18

LOSING ONE'S MARBLES

One of the most scary things — maybe even the scariest thing — about getting old is the prospect of dementia, of losing one's marbles. Old folks to whom this happened used to be referred to as being senile. Now they're said to have Alzheimer's disease. By any name, and to one degree or another, it means losing your mind, and there are few things in life more heartbreaking, especially for those forced to witness the deterioration of a loved one's grip on reality.

In one of his long-ago routines comedian Bill Cosby told audiences about a presumably imaginary relative — an uncle, perhaps, or maybe a grandfather — who was, as the expression goes, "out of it." Cosby would describe a few bizarre things this demented old man tended to do, and then he'd describe the old guy's family's reactions and their concerns about him. But as Cosby pointed out, the uncle or grandfather — whatever — couldn't care less; unmindful of what he had done, he was a happy, smiling man. His dementia wasn't tragic to him, only to those who cared for and about him. There may have been a time when in the initial stages of his dementia the old fellow was aware of losing it, and it had to be, surely, a devastating realization. But once he "progressed" to the edge and slipped over it, serenity took over. His consciousness became banked, and although Cosby didn't tell his audiences so, presumably it eventually would shut down altogether to the extent he'd return to virtual infancy, diaper-clad and spoon-fed, "living" from one day to the next in an adult nursery called a nursing home.

The prospect of that happening, of that progression, is chilling, and any old guy who says he never gives it a thought is lying. And whenever that, or something like that — something really grim — threatens us we tend to make light of it. Thus we pass off and laugh about our brief lapses of memory, calling them "senior moments." We tend to shake our heads when we can't find the car keys, or our seemingly misplaced eyeglasses. A comedy cliché is the old guy in the center of a room trying to remember why he entered it. Young or old, we've all had such experiences, but as the years really begin to pile up such occasions become less and less amusing.

I had the good fortune of knowing and for a brief period living with my maternal grandfather. A Yorkshireman, he was a Victorian orphan who ran away to sea at age fifteen, and before settling in this country had visited most of the world's major ports. He smoked Granger Rough Cut pipe tobacco and I found him fascinating. It was he who when I was about ten or so turned me on to becoming a serious and dedicated reader. He read to me such things as "Two Years before the Mast," "The Adventures of Robin Hood," "David Copperfield," and a once-was classic entitled "Two Little Savages." Unfortunately, he wasn't with my family long. My mother was his youngest daughter, and when the old fellow seemed to be no longer capable of properly caring for himself he came to live with us. My father was fond of him, and the old gent's presence was welcome, especially by me. He talked to me, we'd go for walks together, and, as I've indicated, he instilled in me a love of reading. And then our association ended. Quickly.

He'd arise in the morning, go about his ablutions, get dressed, have breakfast, and then walk a short distance to the village center to buy a newspaper. One morning he didn't return and was found hours later wandering along a country road, unmindful of where he was or how he had managed to get there. The pattern was repeated with increasing frequency, one memorable occasion being when he was returned home in the truck of a road repairing crew. The last straw occurred when one morning, after shaving, he left the water running in an upper floor bathroom basin and neglected to open its drain, the result being a flooded and collapsed ceiling of the room below. Reluctantly my mother had to place him in a home for retired firefighters, and there he died a year or so later. He was well into his eighties.

I relate this because it made a very large impression on me, made me aware that all of us, presumably normal in every respect throughout most of our lives, nonetheless are subject to the possibility and the terrible devastation of losing our minds. That being so, what can be done about it? Not much, as it turns out, although we're told the battle against Alzheimer's is making progress day by day. One indication of this is that an ever-increasing number of doctors and allied medical specialists are turning their attention to gerontology. What we can do is make contingency plans in the event we start to slip off into the fog of old age dementia.

If you or your family can afford a nursing home, scout around for a good one, one that enjoys a good reputation. If you have a friend or friends in such an institution, visit them from time to time. Note how they seem to be getting on, whether they look properly nourished, properly cared for. Are they clean, and are their bed linens clean? Is the smell of urine pervasive? Are the floors clean, the halls well lighted? Are there staff members with whom your friend jokes, or for whom he or she appears to be a pet? What's the food like? Is there a solarium in which you and your friend can visit? Are there amenities available, whether or not they're taken advantage of? How strict are the rules? And so on, all things to be considered in your contingency plan.

Surely you're heard this one:

After it becomes apparent he no longer can take care of himself properly, and after much family discussion, dad agrees to enter a nursing home. Upon his arrival at the home his son sees him to what is to be the old fellow's room. Then the son leaves for the front desk to make a couple of additional arrangements and sign a few papers, assuring his father he'll be right back. The old guy looks out the window, looks around the room, decides it isn't going to be too bad after all, then sits on the edge of what is to be his bed. A minute or so later he starts to lean to one side, and just as he does an attendant walks by and glances in. Seeing the old fellow leaning over, the attendant rushes in and sets him upright and asks if he's okay. Assured all is well, the attendant leaves. Again the old fellow starts to lean to one side, and again a passing attendant uprights him, asks if he's okay, then leaves. Whereupon the son returns and asks, "Well, Dad, what do you think? Think you're going to like it here?" The old fellow says yes, but that the staff seems terribly strict. Asked what he means, he says, "Why, they won't even let you fart."

If you're not going to be able to afford a private nursing home, whether through savings, appropriate insurance, or family support, you're going to become a public charge, and as such are going to have to cope with what your community or state sees fit to provide. Some communities and states do reasonably well by their indigent old people, others couldn't care less (or so it seems). It behooves you, then, to find out all you can before such a need arises; i.e., location, the services provided, the costs (if any) involved, the food served, visitor policy and hours . . . anything pertaining to your being a patient in an essentially public-supported facility.

If you wind up in such an institution you'll probably be asked to, even be required to hand over any income you receive — Social Security, pension, income from property or investments, in other words pretty much "all your worldly goods." That in mind, before you really start going downhill it's a good idea to get together with a trusted attorney and determine how best to cope both with the tax man and to parse out whatever assets you may have. As alluded to above, this process may compel you to forego the legacy you may have planned for your heir(s). However, if it's a matter of you receiving minimum care or leaving the kids money or property, provide first for Ol' No. 1.

Paramount in all of this is the absolute need to discuss in detail with your wife or children (assuming you have either one or both, anyway an heir or heirs) what's to be done when and if dear old dad finally slips over the edge into permanent dementia. Don't be put off by semi-embarrassed protestations that "We'll talk about that when the time comes." The unfortunate fact is that "the time," when it comes, can arrive with startling rapidity, by which time many if not all of your waking hours are spent in mental left field and you'll no longer have a meaningful role in any discussion regarding what's to become of you.

When and if you're first diagnosed with incipient Alzheimer's, gather the pertinent players together and tell them right out why they're there and what's at stake. Be frank in your assessment of your condition and your prognosis. This is no time to be coy, no time to be an all-wise patriarch. Rather it's a time to be an old man facing an abyss, and what you want from them is an honestly arrived at plan to deal with it as gracefully as possible. Too, it might be the time to make a living will, a legal document that empowers one or more people you trust to see to your care and welfare when you become incapacitated. Keep such a gathering within the family; whatever is decided upon or not can later be gone over with an attorney, your bank, investment counselor . . . whatever . . . any trusted person who knows you and knows your business.

Above all, make certain you have an up-to-date will pertaining to your estate, to whatever money and/or property you leave behind, and that those who should know do know where it can be found. At one time my late brother was a judge of probate, and while he never named names, his accounts of some of the messes and estrangements resulting from someone having died intestate defy belief. If you've lived long enough to be an old guy and haven't had your head in the sand throughout, you know that money or the prospect of money can do funny things to people, even those to whom you feel yourself to be closest. Don't kid yourself that a much loved and caring son or daughter is incapable of becoming a fire-breathing dragon should there be enough money at stake. To avoid even the possibility of that happening, line up all your ducks before you check out, whether in death or in dementia.

19

CURTAIN DESCENDING

No one can tell us what it's like to die. A number of doctors, writers, philosophers and other presumably accredited worthies have attempted to do so, but all of them have lacked that one all-encompassing insight — first-hand experience.

Many people have thought they were going to die but either recovered, were rescued or otherwise spared, and their subsequent testimony may be suspect. The man on his death bed who recovers, presumably miraculously, and later assures listeners that at the point of checking out, when his life force was at its lowest ebb, he saw Saint Peter at the Golden Gate more than likely is reflecting the indoctrination, direct and indirect, he has received since childhood. "A band of angels coming after me," or life eternal in the presence of deceased loved ones under the wing of some form of benign deity may be an appealing and comforting thought, but it has the same degree of reality as do the Tooth Fairy and the Easter Bunny.

Given our druthers, I would guess most of us hope to go to sleep in our own bed some night and not wake up. But that, too, is only a hope. Most of us will die in a hospital, hauled there to stem or at least ease, however temporarily, the ravages of cancer, a malfunctioning heart, failing kidneys, a banging liver, a body smashed by calamity, or of pneumonia, the latter often referred to as "the old peoples friend." A number of us will simply crumple, keel over, felled by massive and sudden coronaries or brain hemorrhages; there'll be sudden dizziness, perhaps, or a sharp stab of chest pain, and then *sayonara*. Still others of us will die violently in car crashes, by falling off ladders, from gunshot wounds, in hurricanes, tornados, blizzards, floods, perhaps even as non-combatant war casualties. Regardless of how we check out, it's not something to which we look forward.

On the other hand, many of us, sick and dying and fed up with the whole business, want to get it over with as expeditiously as possible. Not for us the artificial and essentially demeaning life-support systems, not for us heroic efforts to keep us "alive." Thanks to maudlin sentimentality, society spends inordinate sums to keep worn out hearts beating, to keep inhaling and exhaling, often artificially, the corporeal remains of what once were viable human beings. Why? Because we're incapable of simply letting go of those for whom we care? Because the death of someone held dear marks a defeat, and defeat is something we can't abide? Because death deprives us of a certain connection to, a certain verification of, our own lives?

That's probably getting close to it; death of a family member, of a dear friend, is a pointed reminder of our own mortality, and until we personally get to the edge of the cliff it's a reminder we'd rather not entertain. Dick Dempewolff, a lifelong magazine writer and editor, a man of great good humor and a dear and now departed friend, used to say, "Death is Nature's way of telling us to slow down."

Despite all the benefits of modern medicine, all of the hospices, all the programs designed to "ease us over the bar," as it were, dying is a singularly personal thing to do. No one, really, can make the process any less stark and real than it is. Pain can be eased, consciousness suspended, but there comes, inevitably, the moment that in bullfighting is known as "the moment of truth" (in theory, for the bull, but potentially for the matador as well), and we either are or are not aware of its arrival. If unobserved the often heard "He died in his sleep" may account for only a fraction of what transpired. It may simply be equivalent to the flattening out of the wavy line on an oscilloscope, or he may have been roused to some form of consciousness, realized it was just one or two steps to the edge of the cliff, and either fought momentarily or accepted his inevitable tumble into the abyss.

A writer friend of mine named Charles Fox has written brilliantly of his near-death experience. On assignment from *Car & Driver* magazine, he crashed a Lola race car he was driving into a tree at 125 miles-per-hour. He saw the accident as it was happening, knew he was going to die (insofar as he was concerned had already died) yet experienced an out-of-body sensation he referred to as "the silver thread" that enabled him, from a height of about twenty feet, to observe the accident's aftermath. There had been an explosion of aluminum and fiberglass, a warm flash, stillness, and then nothing, just him looking down and seeing his inert body crumpled behind the steering wheel, a body he rejoined to ask an approaching rescuer, "Can I get out now?"

On his death bed, Goethe is supposed to have said, "More light!" and perhaps that's what being conscious of dying is — a fading to black. Whatever it is it can't be dodged, and there's no point in brooding about it. It will happen when it does, period, and about all we can do is hope the hurt stops.

Other than the drawing up of a valid will and the distribution of cherished things, I have a tough time accepting any of the so-called preparations for death. I can't conceive of people buying burial plots, selecting headstones and specifying what's to be chiseled thereon, selecting the music to be played, the verses to be read at their funerals or memorial services. To me that sort of thing smacks of unbelievable vanity. What in the world makes us think our soon-to-be moldering carcass is worthy of such advanced planning? We reach the end of the line, period, and we should get off as simply and as gracefully as possible.

ENDNOTE

Put in touch by a friend of a friend, and as you can tell, one of the old guys with whom I spoke when writing what follows was revered and much-honored comedian Sid Caesar. He's 85, lives in Beverly Hills, and these days keeps a rather low profile, not by choice, perhaps, but thanks to a degree of frailty, years of knockabout comedy presumably accounting for somewhat out of the ordinary wear and tear.

He was most cordial during our telephone conversations and I felt an immediate affinity, perhaps strengthened by our being within three years of each other in age (I'm 82) and both having spent our formative years in two New York City suburbs, he in Yonkers, me in nearby Ardsley.

In a subsequent letter I told him of being occasionally driven to Yonkers by my father, ostensibly for a haircut for me but really so the Old Man could stop by a certain speakeasy, both barber shop and speak I recall being located just off that city's Getty Square. I'd get a haircut while Pop got a couple of belts, and we'd both go home the better for it.

In the letter I couldn't resist an impulse of TV fandom, telling Caesar of a mental picture I've cherished for years.

He was doing an opera skit in his famous bogus Italian, him playing the king, Carl Reiner the scheming Prince Evilo, and I believe Pat Carroll as his queen, who supposedly has given birth to a son she brings forth to show him. The king, swelling with pride, asks the child's name, and when told he skips a couple of beats and in an all-time, world-class double take bellows, "*Sheldon?*"

In my last newspaper job one of my fellow newsroom denizens was a guy named Sheldon, and I was never able to take note of or speak with him without the image of that epic double take flashing in my mind and bringing a smile to my face.

Recalling Sid Caesar's comedy does that for a lot of people.

Did you like HOW TO BE AN OLD GUY?

Do you need more copies for friends and relatives? Of course you do! Also, you may be interested in our other books and gifts:

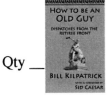

Qty __ *How to Be an Old Guy: Dispatches From the Retiree Front* by Bill Kilpatrick - $19.95

This book covers the issues and transition that men face when moving from work to retirement. With a foreword by Sid Caesar.

Qty __ *SeniorSex: Answers to Your Questions from a Geriatric Gynecologist* by Daniel Laury, M.D. - $19.95

This book provides the answers to sexual questions that patients are seeking from their doctors, and is ideal for single seniors and senior couples, as well as doctors and other medical personnel.

Qty __ *Seniors in Love: A Second Chance for Single, Divorced and Widowed Seniors* by Robert Wolley - $19.95

This well-reviewed book deals with the emotional, financial, physical, and other relevant issues facing seniors when considering a new, intimate relationship.

Qty __ *The Greatest Companion: Reflections on Life, Love and Marriage After 60* by Robert Wolley - $19.95

Through prose and poetry, this book explores the joys of late-in-life love, provides reminders of what such a love needs to flourish, and reflects upon love's agelessness.

Mom No More: Coping With the Late-Life Loss of Adult Children - One Woman's Story by Mignon Matthews - $29.95

The author lost both of her children after they were adults - her daughter Evie at 18 and her son Albert at 42. This is her story of coping with the depression, pain, anger, and injustice of outliving her beloved children.

Sidewalks in the Jungle: What it's REALLY Like to Retire and Live in Costa Rica by Alfred Stites - $35.95

This book deals with the reality of moving to, and living in htis beautiful and stable Central American democracy. Topics covered span from managing maids and gardeners to trips to the doctor and avoiding violent street crime.

The Healthy Seniors Cookbook: Ideal Meals and Menus for People Over Sixty (Or Any Age) by Marilyn McFarlane - $19.95

Whether cooking for yourself, your spouse, or visiting grandchildren, this book features an easy-to-read, easy-to-use format that provides flavorful meals and simple, fast cooking methods.

ABC's for Seniors: Successful Aging Wisdom from an Outrageous Gerontologist by Ruth Jacobs - $19.95

In this book, Dr. Jacobs presents the essentials that enable a reader to harvest life fully for creative, healthy, successful, vigorous, and meaningful aging.

Qty —  *Seniors in Love* car magnet - $11.95
Show the world that love knows no age! An ideal wedding or anniversary gift! Measures six by four inches, in red, white, and gold. Removable. Fits any RV!

Qty — *"Grow old along with me"* mug - $9.95
Robert Browning said it, but it's as true today as it was 100 years ago! Illustration and quote, printed in black on both sides. Truly, *"the best is yet to be"*

Name _____

Address _____

City/State/Zip _____

Please mark the products you want, and their quantity (Missouri residents only please add 5.25% sales tax).

There is no charge for shipping and handling, and all orders are shipped from Greentop, Missouri (population 427).

Send check or money order to:
Hatala Geroproducts
PO Box 42
Greentop, MO 63546

What makes Hatala Geroproducts different?

Hatala Geroproducts of Greentop, Missouri, was founded in 2002. An independent company, Hatala Geroproducts publishes books, games, magnetic signs, and greeting cards primarily for seniors. The focus is on relationships: with spouses, lovers, other seniors, grandchildren, and adult children.

• All products are "age positive," which means that they are respectful to seniors, and focus on the positive aspects of aging.

• All books are "larger print" for easier reading.

• Books are written by senior authors for senior readers.

• All products are developed with the help of academic gerontologists and seniors themselves.

• Hatala Geroproducts is dedicated to remain an earth-friendly, sustainable, carbon-neutral company.

We thank you for your continued support!

If you have any questions or comments, feel free to contact me personally at mark@geroproducts.com

Mark Hatala, Ph.D.
President, Hatala Geroproducts
Professor of Psychology, Truman State University

CPSIA information can be obtained at www.ICGtesting.com
Printed in the USA
LVOW07s1733310315

432750LV00002B/287/P